Kathleen Kelley-Lainé is a psychoanalyst. She was born in Hungary, and her interest in people with the 'Peter Pan' syndrome comes from her own childhood experience of fleeing from her Communist-run country to the West and having to remake her life. She is a naturalized Canadian and lives in France.

Peter Pan

THE STORY OF
A LOST CHILDHOOD

Kathleen Kelley-Lainé

E L E M E N T
Shaftesbury, Dorset · Rockport, Massachusetts
Melbourne, Victoria

The extracts from *Peter Pan* are used by kind
permission of Great Ormond Street Children's Hospital

© Element Books Limited 1997
Text © Calmann-Lévy 1992

First published in Great Britain in 1997 by
Element Books Limited
Shaftesbury, Dorset SP7 8BP

Published in the USA in 1997 by
Element Books, Inc.
PO Box 830, Rockport, MA 01966

Published in Australia in 1997 by
Element Books Limited
for Jacaranda Wiley Limited
33 Park Road, Milton, Brisbane 4064

Translated by Nissim Marshall
Cover Picture courtesy of Great Ormond Street Hospital
Cover design by The Bridgwater Book Company
Page design by Roger Lightfoot
Typeset by WestKey Limited, Falmouth, Cornwall
Printed and bound in Great Britain by Hartnolls, Bodmin, Cornwall

British Library Cataloguing in Publication
data available

Library of Congress Cataloging in Publication
data available

ISBN 1-86204-009-5

Contents

Preface

Most people today believe that the story of Peter Pan was written by Walt Disney and ignore the true author, James Matthew Barrie, a Scottish playwright who made Peter Pan the talisman of his life. *Peter Pan*, the story, was conceived in several stages and took on a number of different forms and versions; it was also written as a play for the Llewelyn Davies family, who were close friends of Barrie. Although the idea of a wandering, lost boy who doesn't want to grow up was J M Barrie's personal obsession, it took the form of Peter Pan, as he invented stories for George Llewelyn Davies, a curious and lively four-year-old.

When Barrie was writing *The Little White Bird*, he wove Peter Pan into it, and this is how Barrie tells of the way he and George made up the tale together:

> I ought to mention here that the following is our way with a story: first I tell it to him, and then he tells it to me, the understanding being that it is quite a different story; and then I retell it with his additions, and so we go on until no one could say whether it is more his story or mine. In this story of Peter Pan, for instance, the bald narrative and most of the moral reflections are mine, though not all, for this boy can be a stern moralist; but the interesting bits about the ways and customs of babies in the bird-stage are mostly reminiscences of [his], recalled by pressing his hands to his temples and thinking hard.

The first version of Peter Pan (that I use in this book) then became *Peter Pan in Kensington Gardens*, the story of baby Peter Pan, who, thinking that he is still a bird (everyone knows that babies before they are born are birds), decides to fly out of the nursery window to go back to the island on the Serpentine in Kensington Gardens – the place of his origin. There he meets the fairies and birds who don't make him one of theirs immediately because he no longer looks like a bird, but is in fact a baby. It takes him some time to become accepted; he gives away bits of his nightshirt to the birds for nest-making, and he plays music on his flute for the fairies when they dance. He finally ends up becoming an indispensable figure in the Gardens.

He does, however, miss his mother and asks the fairies to grant him a wish so that he can fly back to see her. He is certain that his mother's window will be open for him, and that he can come and go as he pleases. When he alights on the window, and sees his mother sleeping, there is a tear on her cheek and he knows that the tear is for her lost boy, Peter. He would like to wake her up by giving her a hug to prove that her 'wonderful boy' has returned, but he is drawn by the freedom of the Gardens and decides to go back there just for a little while, just once more . . .

When he is finally convinced that he will go back to his mother, he again asks the fairies to help him fly, and this time he heads straight for the window, certain that it will be the same as before, but the window is barred and he sees another baby lying in his bed. Peter cries desperately for his mother but she does not hear him, and he finally goes back to the Gardens to live forever with the fairies, all the while longing to be able to play like a real child.

His chance to meet a child, and ask her how real children play, comes at last when he meets Maimie, a lively little girl who gets locked in the Gardens at night. He tries to seduce her into staying with him forever, but when he tells her that her mother may not take her back if she stays away, she prefers to return to her home. She comes back in the day with her nanny and leaves Peter her toy goat. We find out in the end that Peter's main activity in the Gardens is to bury dead children – those who fall out of their perambulators when nurse is not looking and remain in the Gardens after lock-out time: 'But how strange for parents, when they hurry into the Gardens at the opening of the gates looking for their lost one, to find the sweetest little tombstone instead. I do hope Peter is not too ready with his spade. It is all rather sad . . .'

On 23 November 1903, J M Barrie began writing the play *Peter and Wendy* which later became *Peter Pan*. In April 1904 he wrote about the play to Maude Adams, an American actress, for whom he intended the part of Wendy. He writes in the letter: 'I have written a play for children, which I don't suppose would be much use in America . . .' However, it was his American agent, Charles Frohman, who accepted the play immediately, changed the title to *Peter Pan* and insisted the role be played by Maude Adams. He was so impatient to see it performed that he decided to invest in a West End production for Christmas of that year before taking it to America. It was a risky business as the play resembled a circus extravaganza with a cast of over 50, including pirates, Indians, wolves, a lion, a crocodile, an eagle, an ostrich, a dog and a 'live fairy' – at least four of the cast were required to fly around the stage in highly complex movements. The play was a terrific success.

The story begins in the nursery of the Darling family; the children, Wendy, Michael and John, are getting ready for bed as the parents, Mr and Mrs Darling, are preparing to go out for dinner to some friends. The nurse Nana, a large St Bernard dog, is trying to keep the children in line. A skirmish ensues when Michael refuses to take his medicine and his father insists by trying to give the example of someone who can take medicine. Michael wants proof of his father's bravado, and tells him to take it too. Mr Darling is not up to such true courage and cheats by giving the medicine to the dog. As the children realize his trickery, they are deeply disappointed, especially Wendy who idolizes her father.

The parents finally leave the house, and the children are in bed, almost asleep, when the curious figure of a boy lands in the middle of the room, with a ball of light flying around above him. He has come to find his shadow that was cut off by Nana as she slammed the window shut one night when he was sitting on the ledge listening to the stories that Mrs Darling told her children. The light is in fact the fairy Tinker Bell, who finds the shadow rolled up in a drawer, and Peter (for the boy is Peter Pan) tries to stick it back on with some soap, and begins to cry when it doesn't work.

His sobs wake Wendy and a dialogue begins between them. Peter tells Wendy that he lives on an island, the 'Never Never Land', where he is captain of the lost boys. He also informs her that he comes regularly to listen to the stories so that he can tell them to the lost boys. He then persuades her that she should come with him to be a 'little mother' to them all, as her head is full of the stories told by her mother. She finally gives in and wakes up her two brothers; Peter teaches them how to fly, and off they go with him to the Never Never Land.

The Never Land is full of pirates, redskins and mermaids, as well as a crocodile who follows Captain Hook, the frightful captain of the pirates. We learn that Hook and the pirates are out to kill Peter Pan and the lost boys because Peter cut off Hook's hand in a duel and threw it to the crocodile. Since then the crocodile is hungry for the rest, and follows Hook relentlessly; however, as he has also swallowed a ticking clock, he can be heard from a safe distance.

Wendy, her brothers, the lost boys and Peter set up a little house where they play at being a family (Wendy is mother and Peter is father). All is well until the day that Wendy asks Peter what his real intentions are concerning her. He is frightened by her question, insisting that he sees her as 'mother' and wants to be assured that all is just 'make believe' and not real. At this point, Wendy remembers her own mother and thinks about going home. Peter warns that the window may no longer be open. The thought is enough to decide Wendy and her brothers to leave right away; the lost boys also want a real mother, and everyone starts off for London. Peter stays – he doesn't want to grow up.

Before the party actually leaves the Never Land, they are captured by the pirates and are about to be killed, when Tinker Bell tells Peter, who comes immediately to the rescue. Hook is eaten by the crocodile as a result of the battle. Peter then accompanies everyone to the Darling home.

Mrs Darling is so full of joy to find her children again that she agrees to accept the lost boys as well. Indeed she is willing to adopt Peter Pan. He wants to know whether he must go to school, then to work and become a man – 'Yes, of course,' she says. He will have none of it, he never wants to grow up and decides to fly back to the Never Land. Wendy is very sad to lose Peter, so they agree that he will return once a year to take her to the island for spring-cleaning time.

He returns in the beginning, and then forgets to come back for several years. In the final scene Wendy is an adult, with her baby girl in a cradle. Peter appears suddenly in the nursery; he is unchanged and expects Wendy to come away with him. When he realizes that she is a woman, he is terrified and wants to turn out the lights. He then decides to begin the story with Wendy's little girl Jane, and then Jane's little girl Margaret . . .

Introduction

I thought at first that writing this book was one of those pursuits that defies any kind of logical explanation. I realized much later that in fact it was my way of digging up an old story that I had buried as a child.

I was reading Freud's *Mourning and Melancholia* while preparing a paper for a conference on childhood depression, and happened to be reading *Peter Pan* to my seven-year-old son in the evenings. Of course I knew *Peter Pan* from my own young days, and the colourful illustrations that had remained engraved in my mind. But suddenly, for the first time, I heard the cries of a sad child behind the gay, innocent and heartless 'figure' of Peter Pan. The sobs were so insistent that I decided to include *Peter Pan* in my presentation to support Freud's theory on depression. Peter Pan was a sad child who enabled James Matthew Barrie, his creator, to mourn his own unhappy childhood. I ignored the fact that this adventure would also permit me to cry at last.

In his article about Leonardo da Vinci, Freud explains that biographers always have a special emotional relationship with their subjects; very personal reasons motivate their choice. Often fearful of these emotions, the biographer ends up by idealizing his hero, making him conform to some childhood model, usually a father figure. He erases any trace of conflict and suffering, so removing any sign of human weakness or imperfection.

The result is often a cold, strange and rigid model, that has no resemblance to a human being, or with whom it is impossible to identify. For Freud this is regrettable, since truth is sacrificed for illusion; the biographer is simply satisfying his childish fantasies and thereby losing a valuable chance to explore the fascinating secrets of human nature.

He, as a psychoanalyst, proposes to analyse Leonardo da Vinci's neurotic character by pointing out the inhibitions, sacrifices and suffering that marked Leonardo's life since his childhood and made him into a 'failure of a man'; for Freud this means paying him homage, as well as advancing his own theories.

To analyse Leonardo he chooses to start with what is most human, a product of his unconscious: a memory from childhood, an archaic memory written down by the painter himself. The event occurred when he was a baby in his crib and a huge bird, a vulture, according to Freud, landed on him and introduced its tail into his mouth. Freud's analysis is passionately interesting. He retraces Leonardo's childhood, divided between two mothers: his baby years, spent with his real mother whom his father divorced shortly after his birth, and his separation from her at the age of five, when his aging father took him away to live with him and his young sterile wife. Freud links Leonardo's experience with *Mona Lisa*'s mysterious smile. On the other hand, Freud does not mention what can be read between the lines of his text; his own identification with Leonardo's love of his mother.

According to Freud, the passionate desire 'to know' has its origins in infantile sexual activity. For the first five years of his life Leonardo must have been the most adored child, whose mother's kisses were destined solely for the little prodigy. We also know that Freud was the first-born son of a passionate young mother and that he was able to transform that first relationship into his search for psychic truth.

What is the truth of any life story?

The challenge of this book is to throw light on what usually remains in the shadows, on the 'dark side of the moon'; a difficult challenge because it is in the very nature of the unconscious to escape knowledge. The psychoanalyst wants to act as the artisan of the unconscious and use this ephemeral matter, seemingly ignored by the individual, and try to create meaning with it.

The moment when the individual discovers the dynamic of his unconscious is a most impressive one. It usually happens unexpectedly, squeezed in between the cracks of associations, when vigilance is relaxed. It opens onto archaic images, even if only for a moment.

We know that these images are meant to retreat, and that to enable us to live our daily lives they must remain hidden; but we also know that to be true to ourselves, we must descend from time to time to this painfully accessible underground of the mind.

To become an artisan of the unconscious means accepting the need to work endlessly on oneself. Freud insisted on the fact that an analyst cannot take his patient further than he himself has gone in overcoming his own complexes and resistances. With each analytic encounter, the therapist is confronted with her own capacity to associate, her own conflicts and her own search for inner truth. For this reason, Freud recommended the practice of self-analysis as a necessity to become and stay an analyst.

This book is about unconscious processes at different levels: the story of *Peter Pan*, like the enigmatic smile of the *Mona Lisa*, is the product of childhood suffering, that of a sad child resisting total breakdown, whose life and work have been built upon the capacity to resist: 'What if death were the greatest of adventures!' cries Peter Pan as he stands on his rock with the waves rising around him.

My motives for exploring Peter Pan's sadness and for analysing James Matthew Barrie were an unconscious attempt to take on the search for my own psychic truth. It is probably easier to look at one's own life history through that of another than to do it directly. This enterprise has lasted many years, probably due to the amount of time it has taken to construct my defences. The road has not been straight. The story of Peter Pan intertwines with that of James Barrie; the story of Peter Pan mixes with my own.

I hope that you the reader, in turn, will accept being carried away by the movement of your own images, and will be able to discover part of your own internal truth.

1

Peter Pan is Born

'Mummy, did you know how to fly when you were little?' The question seemed to come out of the blue, but my son's face was earnest . . . When I was a child I had my own questions to ask, and they were already serious: 'If I wasn't I, who would I be?' 'If I wasn't here, where would I be?' – 'Yes, my darling, I *did* know how to fly'. Perhaps circumstances forced me to learn and never to forget the art of flying, of soaring over life's tragedies until they became so small as to disappear from sight. I dreamt of 'Once upon a time, was there ever a time, perhaps there was never a time'. All Hungarian fairy tales open with these magic words.

Just like the boy Peter Pan, who flew away from home on the day of his birth because he didn't ever want to grow up, I made 'nowhere' my home, and the 'Never Land' my universe. I suppose that I met Peter Pan rather early in life; maybe it was on the day of my birth when my father first held me in his arms and ordained me with his most intimate wishes: 'This is Doctor Kanitz Katalin!'

Words pronounced upon the heads of newborn babes always have great significance; they can sometimes be so important as to determine the entire life of a person. It couldn't have been the word 'doctor' that would have frightened me enough to make me fly away to Kensington Gardens as did Peter Pan on the day he was born. The weight of my father's dreams behind those famous words must have been heavy upon my cradle. Nevertheless I didn't move. After all, I had just arrived and was probably very tired having survived the adventure of birth, and the warmth of his hands felt good; those hands that were to become so very important.

Peter was absolutely convinced that babies are birds before they are born, and that he could still remember how to fly, which is why he decided to slip out of the window . . .

LIKE A BIRD

Well, Peter Pan got out by the window, which had no bars. Standing on the ledge he could see trees far away, which were doubtless the Kensington Gardens, and the moment he saw them he entirely forgot that he was now a little boy in a nightgown, and away he flew, right over the houses to the Gardens. It is wonderful that he could fly without wings, but the place itched tremendously, and perhaps we could all fly if we were as dead-confident-sure of our capacity to do it as was bold Peter Pan that evening.

One of the great advantages of having such power is that it offers the possibility of travelling through time; however, many grown-ups don't dare take the risk of flying around like Peter Pan for fear of falling backwards, into the Never Land.

Peter landed so suddenly in the Gardens that his first reaction was to lie on his back and wriggle his legs in the air. He had already forgotten that he was a human being and honestly thought he was a bird. He could have answered my first question immediately: 'If I wasn't me, who would I be?' 'A bird!'

This confidence in one's ability to fly is often accompanied by a certain lightness of being that facilitates moving from place to place. In principle, when a baby is firmly held in its mother's arms, the sweet feeling of having weight comes on, together with the reassuring impression of becoming a 'me'. Gradually the wings fall off, the baby becomes heavier, and starts its journey in time without wanting to look back constantly. This conviction of 'being' is accompanied by the capacity to feel and to love.

In fact one wonders whether Peter Pan felt anything at all upon his arrival in the Gardens. For example, he had actually to watch the fairies carry their pails to milk the cows before he could realize that he was thirsty. He therefore flew over to the Round Pond with the intention of plunging in his beak, but of course it was only his nose! He did succeed, however, in sipping a little bit of water, but it was not as refreshing as usual. Then he tried a puddle, and fell right into it.

> When a real bird falls in flop, he spreads out his feathers and pecks them dry, but Peter could not remember what was the thing to do and decided rather sulkily to go to sleep on the weeping-beech in the Baby Walk.

A little later terrible noises woke him, but as is often the case with those very 'light' individuals, he was unable to locate where they were coming from. Were they inside or outside his body? In fact he ignored the fact that the terrible noises were his very own sneezes:

> There was something he wanted very much, but, though he knew he wanted it, he could not think what it was. What he wanted so much was his mother to blow his nose, but that never struck him, so he decided to appeal to the fairies for enlightenment. They are reputed to know a good deal.

Babies who are unable to acquire the necessary weight in their mothers' arms, or those for whom the feeling of 'being' is suddenly interrupted by a tragic event, risk becoming sad children who fly around forever looking for a piece of lost childhood.

It is often the case that a sad child, in the effort not to cry over a lost childhood, will also lose his capacity to feel, which is why he can't tell what comes from inside or outside. Like Peter Pan in Kensington Gardens, he ends up asking someone's advice, for example that of a fairy, in order to know what is happening to him.

I once met a little boy who was terribly sad at having lost his childhood, even though no one suspected he was sad, nor that he had lost his childhood. He was constantly drawing aeroplanes, always the same ones. Despite his energetic 'Nos' we were able to talk about his sadness one day, and I even detected a small tear in the corner of his eye. In a few words he told me how unhappy he had been when his parents moved him from the house where he was born; he was still wearing nappies and his mother was already expecting another baby.

He warned me that he didn't want to know where babies came from; we never raised the issue again. Nevertheless from that day on his drawings changed: long sinuous tunnels filled the page; terrible and mysterious conflicts emerged from the underground caverns; and so he let me know that he had landed a little. In leaving the sky, he was able to make contact with some of the feelings inside, while discovering that he could survive the experience.

THE NIGHTGOWN

Peter Pan wanted to escape the fate of a human being so much that he was determined to remain a bird, just like before his birth. Alas, it was not enough simply to have landed in Kensington Gardens; one had also to be accepted by its inhabitants, the fairies. In fact the fairies were afraid of Peter Pan; he seemed so strange in his little white nightgown that as soon as they saw him they fled to all corners of the Gardens.

Seeing the fairies running away in all directions when he tried to speak to them, Peter had to admit at last that there was a problem. He therefore decided to consult the wisest bird in the Gardens, Solomon Caw, to tell him about his problems. Solomon Caw was of invaluable support to Peter Pan as he was able to make him understand that in fact he was not a 'bird' but a little 'human being in a white nightgown'.

'Look at your nightgown, if you don't believe me,' Solomon said; and with staring eyes Peter looked at his nightgown, and then at the sleeping birds. Not one of them wore anything.

'Ruffle your feathers,' said that grim old Solomon, and Peter tried most desperately hard to ruffle his feathers, but he had none. Then he rose up, quaking, and for the first time since he stood on the window-ledge, he remembered a lady who had been very fond of him.

'I think I shall go back to Mother,' he said timidly.

'Goodbye,' replied Solomon Caw with a queer look.

'But Peter hesitated." Why don't you go?' the old one asked politely.

'I suppose,' said Peter huskily, 'I suppose I can still fly?'

'You see he had lost faith.

'Poor little half-and-half!' said Solomon, who was not really hard-hearted. 'You will never be able to fly again, not even on windy days. You must live here on the island always.'

'And never even go to the Kensington Gardens?' Peter asked tragically.

'How could you get across?' said Solomon. He promised very kindly, however, to teach Peter as many of the bird ways as could be learned by one of such an awkward shape.

'Then I shan't be exactly a human?' Peter asked.

'No.'

'Nor exactly a bird?'

'No.'

'What shall I be?'

'You will be a Betwixt-and-Between, Solomon said, and certainly he was a wise old fellow, for that is exactly how it turned out.'

It is sometimes vital to consult someone in order to be reassured of feeling like a 'human being'.

But the best thing Solomon had done was to teach him to have a glad heart. All birds have glad hearts unless you rob their nests and so, as they were the only kind of heart Solomon knew about, it was easy for him to teach Peter how to have one.

Peter's heart was so glad that he felt he must sing all day long, just as the birds sing for joy but, being partly human, he needed an instrument, so he made a pipe of reeds, and he used to sit by the shore of the island of an evening, practising the sigh of the wind and the ripple of the water, and catching handfuls of the shine of the moon. He put them all in his pipe and played them so beautifully that even the birds were deceived, and they would say to each other, 'Was that a fish leaping in the water or was it Peter playing leaping fish on his pipe?'

But as Peter sat by the shore tootling divinely on his pipe he sometimes fell into sad thoughts, and then the music became sad also, and the reason of all this sadness was that he could not reach the Gardens, though he could see them through the arch of the bridge. He knew he could never be a real human again, and scarcely wanted to be one, but oh! how he longed to play as other children play, and of course there is no such lovely place to play in as the Gardens . . .

THE FIRST WISH

The fact that Peter really wanted to see his mother again proved that he was still a little boy. He finally managed to get what he wanted by tricking the fairies into granting his dearest wish: to be able to fly once more so that he could see his mother. The queen fairy tried to discourage him:

'Will the window be open?'

'Of course!' replied Peter, absolutely sure of himself. 'Mother always keeps it open in the hope that I may fly back.'

'How do you know?' they asked, quite surprised, and really, Peter could not explain how he knew.

'I just do know,' he said.

The window was wide open, just as he knew it should be, and in he fluttered, and there was his mother lying asleep. Peter alighted softly on the wooden rail at the foot of the bed and had a good look at her. She lay with her head on her hand, and the hollow in the pillow was like a nest lined with her brown wavy hair. He remembered, though he had long forgotten it, that she always gave her hair a holiday at night. How sweet the frills of her nightgown were! He was very glad she was such a pretty mother.

But she looked sad, and he knew why she looked sad. One of her arms moved as if it wanted to go round something, and he knew what it wanted to go round.

'O Mother!' said Peter to himself. 'If you just knew who is sitting on the rail at the foot of the bed.'

Very gently he patted the little mound that her feet made, and he could see by her face that she liked it. He knew he had but to say 'Mother' ever so softly, and she would wake up. They always wake up at once if it is you that says their name. Then she would give such a joyous cry and squeeze him tight. How nice that would be to him, but oh! how exquisitely delicious it would be to her. That, I am afraid, is how Peter regarded it. In returning to his mother he never doubted that he was giving her the greatest treat a woman can have. Nothing can be more splendid, he thought, than to have a little boy of your own. How proud of him they are! and very right and proper, too.

But why does Peter sit so long on the rail; why does he not tell his mother that he has come back?

I quite shrink from the truth, which is that he sat there in two minds. Sometimes he looked longingly at his mother, and sometimes he looked longingly at the window. Certainly it would be pleasant to be her boy again, but on the other hand, what times those had been in the Gardens! Was he so sure that he should enjoy wearing clothes again? He popped off the bed and opened some drawers to have a look at his old garments. They were still there, but he could not remember how you put them on. The socks, for instance, were they worn on the hands or on the feet? He was about to try one of them on his hand, when he had a great adventure. Perhaps the drawer had creaked; at any rate, his mother woke up, for he heard her say 'Peter', as if it was the most lovely word in the language. He remained sitting on the floor and held his breath, wondering how she knew that he had come back. If she said 'Peter', again, he meant to cry 'Mother' and run to her. But she spoke no more, she made little moans only, and when he next peeped at her she was once more asleep, with tears on her face.

It made Peter very miserable, and what do you think was the first thing he did? Sitting on the rail at the foot of the bed, he played a beautiful lullaby to his mother on his pipe. He had made it up himself out of the way she said 'Peter', and he never stopped playing until she looked happy.

He thought this so clever of him that he could scarcely resist wakening her to hear her say, 'O Peter, how exquisitely you play!' However, as she now seemed comfortable, he again cast looks at the window. You must not think that he meditated flying away and never coming back. He had quite decided to be his mother's boy, but hesitated about beginning tonight . . .

THE PROMISE TO RETURN

Once one has lost the sweet feeling of gravity in mother's arms it is difficult, perhaps impossible, to find it again. But the memory of it persists and one often tries to bring back the sensation. Just like Peter:

> Twice he came back from the window, wanting to kiss his mother, but he feared the delight of it might waken her, so at last he played her a lovely kiss on his pipe, and then he flew back to the Gardens.

Many nights and even months passed before Peter asked the fairies to grant him the wish to fly back again:

> I am not sure that I quite know why he delayed so long. One reason was that he had so many goodbyes to say, not only to his particular friends, but to a hundred favourite spots. Then he had

his last sail, and his very last sail, and his last sail of all, and so on. Again a number of farewell feasts were given in his honour; and another comfortable reason was that, after all, there was no hurry, for his mother would never weary of waiting for him. So when at last he said to them bravely, 'I wish now to go back to mother for ever and always,' they had to tickle his shoulders and let him go.

He went in a hurry in the end, because he had dreamt that his mother was crying, and he knew what was the great thing she cried for, and that a hug from her splendid Peter would quickly make her smile. Oh! he felt sure of it, and so eager was he to be nestling in her arms that this time he flew straight to the window, which was always to be open for him.

But the window was closed, and there were iron bars on it, and peering inside he saw his mother sleeping peacefully with her arm round another little boy.

Peter called, 'Mother! Mother!' but she heard him not; in vain he beat his little limbs against the iron bars. He had to fly back, sobbing, to the Gardens, and he never saw his dear again. What a glorious boy he had meant to be to her! Ah, Peter! we who have made the great mistake, how differently we should all act at the second chance. But Solomon was right – there is no second chance, not for most of us. When we reach the window it is closing time. The iron bars are up for life.

PARENTS' DREAMS

My mother's wishes were firmly anchored even before I was conceived. Her first was for a baby boy, and now she wanted a little girl around whom to wrap her dreams of blue eyes, blonde hair and dancing steps. I was blonde with blue eyes and loved to dance. My weight was well established before arrival and it was only later on that I acquired the lightness of Peter Pan.

My father had certainly been securely held in his mother's arms at birth; after all, he was the first son and one could feel that his sense of 'being' had been firm from the very beginning. And he was charming!

However, I suspect that he met Peter Pan rather early in life, otherwise how could he have used the strategy of 'flight' so often? The first time must have been when he discovered a little brother who had taken his spot in the cradle. Had he wanted to keep his mother to himself forever?

This original wound never quite healed, and indeed opened up again at the birth of his own son. It was so painful that he was unable to set eyes on the little interloper right away. It was therefore much easier, later on, to plant all his dreams in a little daughter.

In her own way, my mother had also met Peter Pan; she was the last daughter of a family of 13 children and for that reason she probably carried less of the burden of her parents' dreams. In her case, she had been the one to steal the place of a little sister who was not quite ready to give up her privileges as 'the baby'. She had been a very merry and charming child until my mother came along; from one day to the next she ceased to smile and sing.

My grandmother must certainly have felt guilty for the sadness of her little one-year-old, for she found it difficult to give all the necessary attention to her newborn under the jealous surveillance of the older sister. Thus developed the family legend of how my mother cried persistently, day and night, in a desperate effort to attract the vital presence of her mother!

Peter Pan is often around when there is the question of life and death; he waits for the right moment to whisk up a child who may have fallen from his perambulator, not having been held sufficiently well. This type of accident is often due to parental neglect, but can also be the result of too much love, and curiously enough the effect is the same.

When she was two years old, my mother had diphtheria, having been left by her sister to sit for hours in a cold and humid corner of the cellar. The next day she was choking to

death; her face was already going black when my grandmother reached down her throat with a wooden spoon and
succeeded in getting rid of some of the thick matter that
blocked the air passage, thus saving her life. She survived,
but forgot her baby words and her first steps; her mother had
to teach her everything all over again. I often heard my
mother say musingly 'What if she had let me die?'

Both my parents had thus met Peter Pan early in life. But
it was perhaps my grandmother who came into closest contact
with him. She had a little sister whose sole passion was to
play 'burials'. She buried everything – her dolls, dead birds,
flies, chicken bones. She was a pale, transparent- looking
creature, and the contrast with my robust, rosy-cheeked little
grandmother was almost scandalous. Little Emikö, despite
her morose character, and eternal 'No, I don't want any' when
it came to eating, was her mother's favourite. She died on her
fourth birthday and no one knew why. During the burial
ceremony my grandmother kept close behind her mother –
was it to make sure not to lose her? Nevertheless she was near
enough to catch those terrible words that remain engraved
forever: 'Why didn't Elizabeth die instead?'

A mother who wishes a death, a mother who saves a life,
is a mother the child cannot leave. It is as if her arms were
not secure: she either holds the child too tightly, or she is
ready to drop it. The child is not free to acquire the feeling
of just 'being', and the dream of a soft mother with whom it
is so good to 'be' remains the child's quest for life.

Even if he perches on the window-sill and tries to fly off,
the child will not be able to tear himself away from the fatal
attraction of that mother, guardian of the tantalizing secret
of life and death.

I have met people who remain on life's window-sill forever, incapable of making a choice; they don't dare to turn
back for fear of meeting the terrible 'she', nor can they live
without her proximity, and experience a veritable addiction
to her substance, like a drug.

Peter Pan found a solution by going to live in the Never Never Land: that cosy little island that probably reminded him of the protection of his mother's arms even though the length of his journey there gave him the impression of having been able to leave her.

There are various ways of entertaining the illusion of having left the 'mother goddess' despite her firm implantation in one's soul. The strategy of 'flight' can take on a number of different forms, but Peter Pan's departures can be readily recognized by their ephemeral nature, as well as by his cocky laughter from the top of a cloud, or simply from around the corner of the street.

One of the principal characteristics of these flights is that the baby is marked for life by the nostalgic desire to be held in its mother's arms in the hope of reliving those strong sensations of the very beginning of life. All these departures are in fact desperate attempts at finding a second chance; especially when the feeling of 'being human' has not been established with sufficient force. Flights such as these are looked upon as great adventures, while in fact the eternal search for lost childhood is a real tragedy.

THE HOUR OF DEPARTURE

We were quite convinced of experiencing one of the greatest adventures the night we left, all four of us, by the window to fly off to a strange land where there would be no more tragedies and where we would live happily ever after. We left our home one wintry night while all the neighbours were still asleep . . . our home that was later to become the Never Never Land of my life.

Why such a sudden flight out of the window? I never dared to ask that question until now. At the time it all seemed very clear and later it became a story that we kept telling ourselves to justify events. With passing years it turned into a souvenir that I would pull out of a drawer whenever someone asked me, 'In fact, where do you come from?'

My father was Jewish. When the Germans arrived in Hungary, some Jews were collected and taken to camps and were never seen again. Others were simply shot and let fall into the Danube.

My mother saw the long lines along the river: it was winter and the water was frozen, and they had to make holes in the ice . . . 'No! No! Please sir, I am too young, I want to live!' The young adolescent's red hair flashed like blood against the grey sky. My mother closed the window, but was never able to forget that picture.

On the day that the superintendent received the instructions to gather all the Jews in our building, everyone had to go outside onto the pavement: women and children were sent to houses with a yellow star and the men to work camps.

It was Christmas. I was two years old. The living room looked especially bare as there was no tree. I remember my mother sitting in the middle of the room on a chair, crying; in her lap was a crumpled paper indicating the labour camp where my father could be found. In a few weeks he would be shipped off to Germany. We could hear the bombs over Budapest, the signal to rush to the basement. My brother put me in a basket and started to run; I must have been very light indeed. I was both frightened and fascinated by the sound of the siren, the bombs and the planes overhead.

All the tenants huddled together against the cold walls of the cellar. I spent my time singing like a bird; some people would smile at the charming child. Nothing could ever happen to me; this was all a great adventure!

One day my brother and I remained alone, running from the flat to the basement; we couldn't find mother. She was too anxious and scrupulous not to have told us where she was going! 'Your parents are dead, your parents are dead', a joyous little voice kept repeating; I never did understand how that little neighbour could have been so happy just then.

My mother had received a message. My father had succeeded in escaping from the camp when they were being transferred to be taken to Germany. He had jumped into the basement window of a factory that happened to be open. The workers chased him out immediately, but the line of prisoners had passed and my father was not missed. He was able to get to Budapest and have a message sent to my mother. A hiding place had to be found; there was no question of coming home.

My mother tried desperately to find a hiding place. The family printing firm was the first obvious place; surely my father's secretary would have a good solution! But it was already closing time and the office was locked up (and fortunately so, for it turned out later that the secretary was a militant Nazi).

My father was waiting for my mother in the shadow of a doorway in the Vaci Utca. Was it really him? He was so thin that his borrowed clothes drowned him. He who was always so elegant and well groomed . . . only his smile had not changed, but there was no time for long embraces; they had to hurry . . . Where to go? Where to hide? 'To your brother, of course . . . no one will suspect anything . . .'

My father spent the rest of the war hidden in a cupboard at his brother-in-law's apartment. Feri knew that he risked both his life and those of his family but he was a very good-hearted man. The day that my father was blown out of his hiding place by the pressure of a bomb dropped nearby he was obliged to go down to the basement with everyone else.

'Here is my cousin who has just come up from the country.' That was how my uncle Feri introduced my father to his neighbours. As he was so well respected no one questioned his word, and that is how my father survived when he was meant to perish.

APU COMES HOME

My father's return home is still vividly engraved in my memory. It must have been around midday as my mother was preparing lunch on the makeshift open fire that served as our wartime kitchen in the courtyard of our building. Other women were also busy preparing food and I spent my time going back and forth between the yard and the street. On one of my trips my eye caught the form of a man walking toward me on the pavement. His steps seemed strangely familiar and suddenly, without knowing why, I found myself running into his open arms . . .

Who was this man? Where had he gone? Why did he come back? Had they lied to me? 'Daddy has left on a trip. Daddy is in the country. Daddy will be back soon . . .' 'Daddy, Daddy, Apu, Apu.'

After that life went back to almost normal, until the day when it was the Russians' turn to go after my father. They needed a certain number of Hungarian prisoners to take back to Russia. After all, this country had sided with the Germans.

They started rounding up people all over the city. They came to people's apartments in the middle of the night for unknown reasons. They used the same methods as the Germans, only this time the reasons were that of 'class' and not of 'race'. But we were the target once again. Despite the seeming normality of everyday life, my father was increasingly anxious about the menace of 'history'.

It became clear that we had to leave, run, escape, fly away. My father was used to it, only this time he had his family with him. That year we had an exceptional Christmas. The little Jesus was especially generous to me: a beautiful doll, a crib, books and a magnificent pen for my first written words. A gloriously decorated tree reached the ceiling of our apartment. Granny had made more beiglis than usual, those delicious traditional Hungarian nut and poppy-seed cakes that I adored. My mother wore a silk dress and smelled of the sweet French perfume that my father had bought for her in Paris. My father was looking at us; was it worry that had robbed his smile?

A few days later he announced that we were leaving on a winter holiday. It was as unexpected and brutal as the day that he announced that we had changed our name. This event occurred, I must admit, following an incident in my school. The teacher called me 'that Kanitz girl . . .' with so much hate in her voice that I asked my father why we had such an ugly name. Two days later our name was 'Christianized' to Kelley. My mother was not happy: the war was over; it is true that some Jews had changed their name as an attempt to escape the Nazis' final solution, but why do it in 1949, after all that we had been through!

TRAVELLING LIGHT

Before leaving my father told us that we could not take much baggage; no dolls, no crib, no books, even my new pen remained on the table. I had to be very light on this vacation; I chose to take only my little rabbit. Years later I understood that this little rabbit represented a moment of great happiness in my childhood: on my fifth birthday my parents woke me up with this gift. They were smiling and I felt enveloped by their love, the warmth of their presence; I knew that I was happy!

The suitcases were soon ready. A black car was waiting for us in the street. No one used cars very much at that time, and it seemed very odd that we should be affording this luxury. It was night, but the stars were not shining as brightly as on the Christmas eve that my brother took me out for a walk in the snow while our parents decorated the tree . . . I took a last look back at our windows, and imagined letting my fingers run around the wrought-iron trimming of the balcony. The same feeling returned many years later when I saw our house again.

I hugged my little rabbit very tightly and felt sad about leaving my new doll alone, even if it was only for a short vacation.

Before leaving Budapest, we stopped at the home of some people I didn't know. Their faces were very serious; a woman dressed in black spoke to my mother about things that I couldn't understand. We had to leave our suitcases at their place.

'Of course we will send you all your valuable objects . . . of course . . .'

'Come here, little one, give me your rabbit, my son will keep it for you.' The woman in black smiled at me knowingly.

My mother did not hear my desperate, silent cry. I needed her protection, I wanted her to save my rabbit, I wanted her to put out her arms to stave off the disaster . . . but she was absent, her look was empty. For the first time in my life I felt completely alone, and helpless. I had to give up my rabbit.

Our next stop was in the country, in the basement of someone's house. A number of men were gathered there and we had to wait for others. My father warned me not to speak out loud since the owners of the house did not know that we were there. What an adventure!

A little later we split into two groups. It was agreed that my father and brother would continue by bicycle; my mother and I, disguised as peasants from the country, the customary scarves tied under the chin, were to take a bus with another lady. If anyone should ask me a question, I was to say that the lady was my mother and my mother was my aunt. I didn't understand a thing, and yet somehow I understood it all. The Hungarian countryside rushed by the windows of the bus, and the wheels were singing 'goodbye, goodbye, goodbye . . .'

We arrived at a large farm. There were a thousand things for a city child like myself to discover, but I was told not to play: 'Stay close to the house, and if you see a mounted policeman come in immediately. Take the gold chain off from around your neck, it could attract attention.'

I chased the geese and ducks until two men in uniform stopped me short. My heart started to pound and I ran to find my mother; she turned as white as a sheet.

'Your papers, please!'

My mother fainted and the two men burst into laughter: 'Mrs, you mustn't take things so hard. We have come to help you. It was just a joke, that's all!'

The two jokers were our 'passers', and had just arrived to take us over the border to Austria. It took some time to re-assure my mother; she was never able to laugh about it.

We passed the border that was more like a gutter than a significant political barrier. The electric fencing that later represented the 'iron curtain' had not yet been installed, and all that was needed was a little jump to get to the other side. I thought it was great fun to ride on the shoulders of one of the jokers in uniform who helped us across.

Once we were in Austria, we still had to walk for a long time through fields and forests before reaching our destina-tion, the farm house where we would spend the night. We were very silent, but I seemed to hear my father whisper 'We are free!'

Bowls of warm milk awaited us and the comfort of a friendly farm family did us a lot of good. We all slept in the same large room with the grandfather, his little grandson and the Christmas tree that was still in place. I shared a bed with my mother, and despite the reassuring warmth of her body, I had great difficulty in falling asleep. The next morn-ing she told me that we had left Hungary forever. At last I was able to cry: 'Oh, my doll! Oh my little rabbit, I have lost you; I shall never, never find you again!'

2

Peter Pan on the Window-sill

The freedom to come and go, and to be sure that mother is still waiting, her eyes following the little one from behind the open window . . . these are some of the conditions that are necessary for a child to gain the maximum benefit from childhood, and to have the strength to break away from it one day to grow up at last.

Peter just wanted to go and play with the fairies, but he also wanted to see his mother again, to make sure that she was waiting for him and that he continued to exist in her eyes.

But the window was locked, and when he saw another baby in his bed everything became disorganized. Peter no longer had a mother or a cradle; he experienced the greatest tragedy that can ever happen to a child. He cried desperately as he leaned on the closed bars, thumping his little fists on the pane . . . he had just lost his childhood.

When the border closed behind us, my parents knew that there was no turning back. I cried over the dolls that I had abandoned in the house, those rooms that would no longer be filled with our laughter; but did I know that it was my *childhood* that I was leaving behind at number 20 Mar Jenö Utca?

Even if we do not recognize the weight of such tragedies when they occur, we all have the remnants of very old memories that stay alive despite ourselves. Peter was terribly sad in front of the closed window. The pain he felt in his arms and legs reminded him vaguely of another pain that he had known a very long time ago. Was it a souvenir of a bird? Was it the souvenir of a baby? Or was it something in between?

Was he suddenly feeling the full weight of experience of when he left his nest of origin? It is very difficult for a human being to grow up, because it means abandoning a nest that has been ever so comfortable.

I once watched a mother squirrel teaching her young one to jump from tree to tree. She used a mother's trick: she rubbed her tits close to the little one's nose, pretending she would suckle him, and then she jumped onto the next branch. The little squirrel trembled with fear, but the desire for his mother's warm milk finally gave him the necessary courage to jump higher and higher up the tree.

A MOMENT'S DISTRACTION

Going and coming back also allows us to revisit our old nest from time to time, and reassures us about what we were. Eventually this becomes unnecessary, because what we were in the past has become an integral part of what we are now, in the present.

A mother's first task is to learn how to trick her little one so that he/she does not regret having left the original nest, that is, the mother's tummy. Generally mothers are ready for this job right away and in fact are adept at giving cuddles and looks that make babies forget rather quickly that they were birds.

Perhaps Peter's mother was unable to do just that, and that is why he left so quickly out of the window. On the other hand, he didn't really give her much time. Some mothers need a lot of time: for even if they have been expecting the little bird with passion, when he finally does arrive, they are unable to do what it takes to make him not regret leaving the nest.

It is also a moment when mothers tend to remember the time when they were little birds. Sometimes they even forget that they have a little one of their own who is waiting. Perhaps it was one of these moments, when his mother was not looking, that Peter flew out of the window for the first time. When he told the story to Wendy, he said it was because his mother had forgotten to weigh him. It certainly is true that one must weigh babies as soon as they arrive, to give them the weight that will keep them from flying off.

The question of weight is an important and serious one. When a child has had to live through heavy tragedies too early on in life, rather than weighing in his own body, the weight presses so heavily on his past that he is obliged to fly off to escape being crushed. If the weight is a tomb, it is even more difficult to carry.

This is why you can recognize a sad child by his extreme lightness of being, either in body or mind. Clowns are among the saddest persons on earth.

When the window is barred, and when borders are wired with electric fencing, there is no turning back; the past takes on heaviness, a kind of gravity that melts into some distant paradise lost of one's childhood origins. The child, in an attempt to gain lightness, lets go of many attributes, including having to choose his/her sexuality.

Being a girl or boy is a very heavy responsibility for a sad child, much more difficult than being both at once or nothing at all. Choosing one's sexuality means agreeing to grow up and accepting the prospect of dying one day. Angels, for example, are not sexual beings; they have wings instead.

THE ADVENTURE OF GROWING UP!

Peter had to give up going back to his mother; he felt desperately wounded, and as he returned to Kensington Gardens he decided never to say the word 'Mother' again.

Suddenly the Gardens had lost all their attractiveness to him; he could not play as before, and even the fairies could not cheer him up. Only Tinker Bell, the most amusing of all the fairies, was able to raise his interest from time to time.

She told him wonderful stories about the Never Never Land, and that is how he decided to go and live there and have endless adventures with the pirates and Indians and the 'lost boys' who had fallen out of their perambulators when nurse was not looking. He decided to become their leader. The adventures of Peter Pan begin as follows:

> All children, except one, grow up. They soon know that they will grow up, and the way Wendy knew was this. One day when she was two years old she was playing in a garden, and she plucked another flower and ran with it to her mother. I suppose she must have looked rather delightful, for Mrs Darling put her hand to her heart and cried, 'Oh, why can't you remain like this forever!' This was all that passed between them on the subject, but henceforth Wendy knew that she must grow up. You always know after you are two. Two is the beginning of the end.

The story of Peter Pan is the story of a sad child, a child so sad that he refused to grow up. Usually stories tell you how to grow up; Peter Pan tells you how to stay in one place for ever, how to live in the Never Never Land.

THE DARLING FAMILY'S WINDOW

Despite all the fascinating adventures he had in the Never Never Land, Peter Pan still felt the need to journey to London from time to time. In fact he was motivated by what he felt to be a kind of nostalgic yearning among the lost boys for stories and fairy tales. Peter therefore decided to fly regularly to London and sit on the window-sill of a real family and listen to a real mother telling stories to real children. This is how he landed one evening at the Darling family at No 14:

Mr and Mrs Darling and their three children, Wendy, the eldest daughter, and the two boys Michael and John.

When you come to know Peter Pan, you can imagine that he didn't land on that particular window by chance. Even if the Darling family seems to be just an ordinary English family at first sight, there must have been a little crack that Peter could slide into, otherwise how could he have exerted so much influence on them, as we will see later on.

Let us begin with Mrs Darling.

She was a lovely lady with a romantic mind and such a sweet mocking mouth. Her romantic mind was like the tiny boxes, one within the other, that come from the puzzling East; however many you discover there is always one more.

Mrs Darling was one of those women who you can never really know completely. Was Peter Pan hiding in one of those boxes? In any case the kiss that was on the right-hand corner of her sweet mocking mouth and that her daughter Wendy could never get, was certainly for him!

Mrs Darling first heard of Peter when she was tidying up her children's minds. It is the nightly custom of every good mother after her children are asleep to rummage in their minds and put things straight for next morning, repacking into their proper places the many articles that have wandered during the day.

On her knees she lingers humorously over some of the contents wondering where her children picked this up, making discoveries sweet and not so sweet, pressing this to her cheek as if it were as nice as a kitten, and hurriedly stowing that out of sight. When her children wake in the morning, the naughtiness and evil passions with which they went to bed have been folded up small and placed at the bottom of their minds; and on the top, beautifully aired, are spread the prettier thoughts ready to be put on the next day.

MOTHERS' WISHES

I know that all mothers tend to rummage around in their children's heads, but Mrs Darling was so intent on putting her little one's thoughts in order that one may suspect she feared losing them. After all, she had so wanted to have children, even against her husband's wishes!

It is customary for mothers to plan their babies in collaboration with their husbands. Sometimes they are so anxious to leave nothing to chance that they start drawing their babies so that they can control all their features: the nose, the mouth, the eyes. They often have someone in mind: a sister, a brother, a grandfather: it may be in hope of keeping the child the same forever. We saw how Mrs Darling was in the garden with her little two-year-old daughter: the child was so deliciously beautiful as she ran towards her mother to offer her a flower, that she pronounced these terrible words: 'Oh, if you could only stay like this forever!'

Such nostalgic wishes 'if only' can have very contradictory effects on a child: sometimes it is precisely those words that make him/her understand (as did Wendy), that one must grow up. At other times it works, and the child does not grow.

It can happen that a sad child has the unconscious feeling that he/she must not develop beyond a certain age. I met a mother who had lost a child of three in an accident. Many years later she gave birth to another boy who resembled the dead child so much that she had the impression that the dead one had come back. The second boy became a sad child at three; he had reached the same age as his dead brother and felt that he must not go beyond this point, otherwise his mother would no longer love him.

Mothers who so want their child not to grow up tend to hang on to their 'status' as mother. Being a mother is one way of finding one's own mother: the one that is lost, the one that one never had, the one that one would have liked to have had.

The little girl inside Mrs Darling was probably still very close to the surface, ready to pop out at any time and wanting to make her feelings heard. To find Peter Pan again was her way of finding her lost childhood. But that encounter was to have a high price.

Looking for that lost boy, she constantly bumped into him in the thoughts of her children. The word 'Peter' was coming back and she couldn't understand why; she knew no one by that name. But when she remembered her own childhood it all came back. They used to tell strange stories about him, for example that when a child died, he used to accompany him for part of the way so that he wouldn't be afraid. She used to believe that he really existed at the time, but now that she was married and full of good sense, she had serious doubts:

'Furthermore,' she said to Wendy, 'he must have grown up by now.'

'Oh no, he hasn't grown up,' assured Wendy with great conviction, 'he is exactly my size .'

Mrs Darling consulted Mr Darling but he just smiled ironically: 'It is surely those silly things that Nana puts into their heads; that's what you get for having a dog for a nurse, it is just like the sort of idea that she would have! Stop talking to them about it and it will go away.'

But 'it' didn't go away, and soon that troublesome boy came to cause Mrs Darling a real shock.

THE POWER OF A DREAM

Children are capable of having the strangest adventures without batting an eyelid. For example, they can tell you a story about their father one week after his death: that they met him in the forest, having set him a trap and it was such great fun! At that moment death is no problem for them; it has no weight.

An attentive mother knows how to compensate such extreme lightness of being in her children. Mrs Darling,
however, was too much involved in 'once upon a time . . .'

While she was asleep, she had a dream. She dreamt that the
Never Land had come too near and that a strange boy had
broken through from it. He did not alarm her, for she thought
she had seen him before in the faces of many women who have
no children. Perhaps he is to be found in the faces of some
mothers also. But in her dream he had rent the film that obscures
the Never Land, and she saw Wendy and John and Michael
peeping through the gap.

The dream by itself would have been a trifle, but while she
was dreaming the window of the nursery blew open, and a boy
did drop on the floor. He was accompanied by a strange light,
no bigger than your fist, which darted about the room like a
living thing; and I think it must have been this light that wak-
ened Mrs Darling.

She started up with a cry, and saw the boy, and somehow she
knew at once that he was Peter Pan. If you or I or Wendy had
been there we should have seen that he was very like Mrs
Darling's kiss. He was a lovely boy, clad in skeleton leaves and
the juices that ooze out of trees; but the most entrancing thing
about him was that he had all his first teeth. When he saw she
was a grown-up, he gnashed the little pearls at her.

Mrs Darling screamed and, as if in answer to a bell, the door
opened and Nana entered, returned from her evening out. She
growled and sprang at the boy, who leapt lightly through the
window. Again Mrs Darling screamed, this time in distress for
him, for she thought he was killed, and she ran down into the
street to look for his little body, but it was not there; and she
looked up, and in the black night she could see nothing but what
she thought was a shooting star . . .

She returned to the nursery, and found Nana with something
in her mouth, which proved to be the boy's shadow. As he leapt
at the window Nana had closed it quickly, too late to catch him,
but his shadow had not had time to get out; slam went the
window and snapped it off.

You may be sure Mrs Darling examined the shadow carefully,

but it was quite the ordinary kind. She thought of showing it to Mr Darling, but he was totting up winter greatcoats for John and Michael, with a wet towel around his head to keep his brain clear, and it seemed a shame to trouble him.

Therefore she decided to fold up the shadow and put it carefully in the top drawer of the dresser, until she could find the opportune moment to speak of it to Mr Darling.

THE FATHER'S ROLE

Mrs Darling's lost childhood was not enough to let Peter Pan sneak in the window of No 14 if the father, Mr Darling, had been able to protect his family. However it was not the case. Even though his wife had made several attempts to warn him of the danger of this strange person, Mr Darling was too fragile himself, with very low self-esteem, which meant that he was particularly vulnerable to Peter Pan's 'incursions'.

Fathers often find it difficult to find a comfortable place between wife and children, especially when they have not had sufficient support from their own father. A wife can either facilitate the father's role concerning his children or render it very difficult. We noticed that Mrs Darling preferred to draw her children's faces alone, without her husband. Perhaps it was also because Mr Darling was constantly delving into his accounts that he didn't take the time to participate in the construction of his children.

One must know of course that fathers' reasons for counting so ardently is to relieve the anxiety of losing their place when the child arrives. It is particularly true for the first one, and once there are several the battle for the centre of attention becomes a habit. Some fathers leave their families at this time and try to find a central place elsewhere. Others don't leave, but never get used to it and begin counting every time, and Mr Darling was one of these.

Mr Darling was particularly sensitive to what the neighbours thought, for he hoped that their esteem for him would make him feel better about himself. It was because of the neighbours that he felt ashamed of having a dog for a nurse, even though he knew that no nursery could be better kept. After all, he had his place at the City to think of! Furthermore, Nana troubled him in other ways: he sometimes felt that she didn't admire him. ' "I know she admires you tremendously, George," Mrs Darling would assure him, and then she would sign to the children to be specially nice to father.'

The most bothersome of all was Mr Darling's behaviour. Although he was the most discreet and anonymous person outside the home, with his family he just let go, and blew hot and cold without hesitation.

It is often the case that the father of a sad child resembles Mr Darling. Many men have told me how much they had longed for a father capable of supporting them as children throughout their childhood, and the profound deception they felt when they realized that their father was just another child.

Sometimes a child in this situation hangs on to the image of his grandfather. This is what the little pilot who drew aeroplanes did: as he felt deprived of his father, he latched onto his maternal grandfather who became the hero of his life. However, a grandfather is never a father, and the risk for the child is another form of internal disorganization. He can imagine that he is his own father, or that his direct genitor is God.

In fact, it is just this kind of disorganization that allowed Peter Pan to whisk off the Darling children that famous Friday evening. If we observe the scene in a very superficial way we see children playing in the nursery and they don't want to go to bed. Or we know that neither children nor adults play at just anything by chance. If we look again more carefully, we see that this particular evening they were playing at 'mothers and fathers'. Were they attempting to find a better kind of organization than their own parents were able to achieve?

A little lost girl came to tell me about her sadness, for no one wanted to believe that she was intelligent and capable of growing up. Instead of talking to me about what was hurting her, she invented an imaginary family and for years we played the game so intensely that we began believing in the real existence of the family. Each time I tried to ask some questions, proposed an interpretation, she told me to keep quiet. Then the little girl grew.

One day she arrived and just dropped into one of the chairs with a big sigh and, looking me straight in the eye for the first time, said: 'Now I want to speak to you.' That day I realized that she had become an attractive adolescent girl. The play family had allowed her to reorganize her feelings, feelings so confused that they couldn't allow her to grow up.

BETWIXT AND BETWEEN OF DISORGANIZATION

After our escape from Hungary we had to wait several months to achieve my father's cherished goal: to get out of Europe. Despite his deep cultural roots he was convinced that the Fascist trauma would return again and again to the Old Continent, so he wanted to move to the New World, where he thought that totalitarian regimes were unlikely to happen.

This time of waiting for the 'great leap' was quite idyllic for me. No one went to work or school and we did everything together. In this 'betwixt and between', just like Peter Pan, it was possible to imagine everything, to play at everything, to be the sun and the air, night and day, little and big, girl and boy, father and mother.

Our first stop was Vienna. It was evening when we arrived, and my father took us straightaway to his mother's family home; she had been of Viennese origin. It was a large apartment in an old building located on the Friedrichstrasse. Its present owner was Paula (the only survivor of the Munk family), the maid whom Uncle Hugo had married on his deathbed, much to the outrage of the whole family.

Having recovered from her surprise at our arrival, Paula was not too keen to let us stay at her house and so my father had to search for another solution quickly. He thought of the Scout movement to which he belonged. While in London as an adolescent he had come across Baden-Powell, and was inspired to start a Scout group in Hungary with some of his friends. It was thanks to this network that he found places for us to stay. However, we were to be separated once again; my mother and I shared a bed at the home of Ida Kraus, who was a tiny little widow and a fervent Catholic. My father and brother stayed with another family. All of us lost our feelings of security for a while. Are parents in flight still parents?

When parents have the walls, warmth and light of a house to help them create childhood space, their little ones know that even if they wander off, they will still be able to return to their internal home. We were suddenly without a country, without a name and without a home. During our journey we lived in 'borrowed interiors', belonging to those who were willing to share them with us. Happily Ida Kraus' hospitality re-created some of the lost warmth of our home.

My memories of 'tante Ida' remain very clear to this day; I liked her smile, her round face and her small size – I felt she was closer to me than other adults. A particularly fascinating aspect of her apartment was a secret room that she retired to every evening for long periods; it was generally accepted that this room was forbidden to us, and so my joy was all the greater when she invited me into this sacred place. I was in such awe that I had to hold my breath for everything inside was gold, silver and precious stones. There were porcelain dolls in glass cases, and oriental carved wooden boxes of various shapes in all corners of the room. Tante Ida opened one of these and took out a child's ring set with two diamonds and a ruby and gave it to me. I felt very proud. 'When you wear this ring, you will remember me,' she said, smiling warmly. I still have the ring, but the stones have been lost.

Meanwhile my father found people who could help us across the Russian zone into the American zone. Tante Ida's farewell dinner was delicious; she even made a special festive chocolate cake, covered with colourful decorations. It was the first time that I tasted such a cake – it was a change from our 'beigli', which we ate on festive occasions.

FREE ZONE

During the second stage of our journey I was aware of what we were doing, and the risks we were taking. Nevertheless, for me it was still like an adventure in the movies.

It was night when we set out through the woods around Vienna; the road below was filled with Russian soldiers, searching the area for fleeing persons with their powerful spotlights. When the beams came too close to us we stopped and held our breath until they passed by. The road seemed endless, and we arrived in Innsbruck early the next morning. The free zone at last!

In Austria there were refugee camps called 'lagers', a kind of concentration camp for DPs (displaced persons) without a country, without a passport, without an identity. It was quite natural that we should join others who had taken the chance to flee. Nevertheless my parents found the two days we spent in the Innsbruck lager unbearable. We had a small room in the long grey barracks with some very rudimentary kitchen supplies. Everything else was shared with the others. The people were sad and lost, the place was shabby and grey, and my father decided to find another solution. After two days we were installed in a tiny guesthouse in Innsbruck. Our room was at the end of the corridor, shared with a mother cat and her six kittens. I felt happy.

Our next stop was Salzburg, where I spent the best days, and experienced the worst fright, of my life. My father found us a very comfortable hostel in the woody hills outside the city, which belonged to a family with two children. At first my relationship with Hans, who was five years old, and Kristel, who was nine, was very distant, but gradually we grew closer. The four of us did a lot of hiking, exploring the surrounding forest, watching out for animals, picking bunches of wild flowers. My father looked really happy at last, and he played with us constantly. We had a great feeling of freedom; I really hoped that time would stand still there.

I came to know Kristel little by little. She had an impressive collection of toys and dolls and she wore the Austrian 'dirndel', the dress of my dreams that was naturally too expensive for me even to hope for. Unfortunately she also had something that frightened me terribly: her aunt! My father tried to persuade me that she was a very kind woman, but her face was badly deformed by paralysis after a shock, and I was convinced she was a witch; especially the day that I encountered her as if in a nightmare.

It was a quiet afternoon, and Kristel invited me to play with her in her room after lunch. 'Come, let's take my new doll's pram out.' She opened the door of the darkened adjoining room and there, lying on the bed, I could see her aunt! My heart started to race, and my legs weakened. Kristel pushed out the pram; the aunt remained motionless. A few minutes later, however, she came into Kristel's room and advanced directly towards me, holding out her hand to stroke my head and saying 'Kätchen, liebe Kätchen'. I jumped up and ran to the door, trying desperately to open it, pale as a ghost and unable to speak; they let me out at last and I fled to our room. 'Whatever happened?', exclaimed my mother, very surprised. I couldn't reply; I just fainted in her arms.

I have only experienced this extreme kind of fear on one other occasion, when I was in residence at university and found myself in the middle of the hall instead of in bed, not knowing how I had got there. I had dreamt that an enormous spider was bearing down on me, and must have sleep-walked into the hall.

It is often during moments of passage from one state to another, during important changes, like growing up, that old 'witches' come out of their boxes, to remind us of their presence just when we think they have disappeared for good.

A VISA FOR THE FUTURE

In Salzburg we waited for our visas. My father had business contacts in Canada and Australia who had agreed to sponsor us as immigrants. During the years following the war these countries needed extra manpower, and it was quite easy to immigrate as a manual worker. But my father had requested another status. His dream was to introduce Hungarian artists to the New World by printing their work on Christmas or birthday cards, for example. In Canada our 'sponsor' was a Hungarian painter. Our Canadian visa was the first to arrive, and that is how we became citizens of that country.

We still had to cross many countries before reaching the boat for the great voyage. Zürich train station was very clean, even then; everything sparkled. I was fascinated by some strange fruits, laid out on an impeccable little wagon. As there was still some time before the train pulled out of the station, my father got off and bought two bananas for the four of us to share. It was the most delicious banana I had ever had; I could never quite find the same taste again, even in Africa!

Can one *ever* rediscover the tastes of childhood? As the sense of security is lost, the sad child hangs on even more intensely to the tastes, smells and pictures of childhood, in order to conserve just for one more moment those delicious hours when he was surrounded by loving parents and still had the feeling of being able to come and go without getting lost.

Our next stop was France, where my father had some cousins. We arrived in Paris on 14 July 1949, and finding the family made us feel safe again. Furthermore, my father spoke French.

'Pista, why don't you settle in France? Your business contacts are in Europe, you wouldn't be lost here . . .' But my father was determined to proceed with his plans: the way ahead was to go to the New World, to sever his roots and begin all over again. He believed in the promise of a second chance.

Is it possible that I decided then and there, at the age of six, to come back to France one day? We were going to cousin Lucie's for dinner, and did some window-shopping on the way in the elegant Trocadero district. I stopped in front of the most beautiful toy shop I had ever seen. Although I didn't dare to ask for anything, it could not stop me from dreaming . . . and thinking about my dolls, my rabbit, lost forever.

The table was already set when we arrived at Lucie's apartment; we waited for her daughter, Nicole. During the war Nicole had been captured by the Germans and had survived the horrors of the concentration camp. She came back traumatized and her mother was very worried about her. She arrived at last, carrying a large box that she held out to me. 'Here, this is for you . . .'

I was amazed. I opened the box with difficulty for it was beautifully wrapped in coloured paper and I was unused to it; in Hungary we didn't follow the custom of wrapping presents. When I finally untangled the beautiful ribbons and paper to open the box, I couldn't believe my eyes: there was the Little Red Riding Hood doll that I had admired such a short while before in the shop window. I jumped for joy, kissing Nicole and everyone else . . . I no longer felt alone.

This present must have helped a little to heal the childhood wound that I was carrying; I was certain to return to France one day. When finally I did settle in Paris as an adult, it was Nicole who introduced me to the man who was to become my husband and father of our child.

At last the moment arrived when we were to leave Europe for the New World. We went to Le Havre by train and embarked on the Portuguese ship *San Maria* that was to take us, along with a large number of emigrants, to Quebec City. I have no real memory of our departure, of the land moving away slowly and the people getting smaller and smaller, waving their handkerchiefs sadly as the ship set out for the open sea.

I know that the trip was neither luxurious, nor always pleasant. My neighbour in the bunkbed was a small four-year-old Russian boy, who didn't smile much. My lasting memory of him was the way he would chant from morning till night 'Banana, banana!' Was the fascination that we shared for the exotic fruit a sign of our stressful childhood?

The ship took the northern route which passes near Iceland and we faced the danger of icebergs. My father didn't stop moving around on board, talking to everyone. My mother was worried, full of doubts and questions that remained unanswered. She was already nostalgic for all that she had lost. 'Where are we going to live?' 'Where will you work?' 'What are we going to do with the children?'

For my father these were not important questions; everything would take care of itself when we arrived. Only one thing mattered: 'We are free! Do you realize that we are free?'

FROM DREAM TO REALITY

When we arrived in Toronto, our final destination, the welcome was not exactly as my father had expected. Our 'sponsor' was very nice and polite, but he didn't offer us lodgings until we found a place of our own; instead he reserved a suite for us in one of Toronto's most luxurious hotels. We remained there for a week, but my father began worrying about our finances. We were no longer in a provisional state; there was no question of dreaming about other people's homes.

We therefore changed hotels and moved to a much less elegant district and my father began seriously looking for lodgings. It was not easy. Unlike European cities, here many people lived outside the heart of the metropolis in private houses with gardens. It was the poor who lived in shabby buildings in the centre of town. There was also the immigrant area where Polish and Russian Jews lived. Many made a living by running used clothes shops, or food stores where you could buy special pickles and other delicacies from Central Europe.

It was in this district that my father finally found a Hungarian family of peasant origin who had immigrated to Canada in the 1930s, and who rented out rooms in their house. After some lengthy negotiations they agreed to rent to a family with children.

We spent little time in the shabby room; we just cooked our meals and slept there, and that is surely why I have few memories of the place. However, a specific event does come to mind: we were seated at the little table in front of the window having a meal, when suddenly I had an urgent and uncontrollable desire to throw my fork out of the window and see it fly. As a result I received the only slap on the face that my mother ever gave me!

JUMP INTO THE VOID

When a child flees from home with her parents, there is no question of leaving the nursery; there is no longer a nursery, there are no windows, or parents waiting for the child to come back . . . there only remains the memory of the warmth, of the perfume and the light . . . there only remains the dream . . .

Wendy was at that point in her life when the question of leaving the nursery became real. She needed to be reassured of the strength of her parents, especially her father. When children reach this critical stage in life they invent all sorts of tricks for testing parental strength, to make sure that they will be able to count on them. Sometimes parents can't withstand this period of testing, and fall into the trap of becoming children themselves. The disappointment of their offspring can be so great as to be catastrophic, just as with the Darling family.

On that famous yet tragic evening at No 14, the trap was set with such discretion, and seemed so trivial, that Mr Darling didn't realize the seriousness of it all until afterwards. Let us go and observe the scene in detail, and examine the relevance of the participants' words and gestures.

Mrs Darling thinks she sees a little face at the window and is frightened – 'My God, my children!' – but the face disappears; everything is normal, the children are playing in the nursery. However their game is not innocent:

'We are doing an act; we are playing at being you and father,' announces John. (He imitates the only father who has come under his special notice.) 'A little less noise there.'

They play at the most essential scene: parents' desire to have children. Parental desire is not always clear-cut; did they want a girl or a boy? John thinks that one can only want a boy. Wendy is deeply wounded to think that her mother didn't desire her. She thinks that mothers don't care whether it is a boy or a girl, and that they are happy to 'just have a baby!' When it is Michael's, the youngest's, turn, John says with a touch of sadism (he is playing Mr Darling's role): 'We don't want any more children, two is enough!' Michael begs desperately: 'Please John, just one more, John, a boy!' He is frightened by the idea that no one wants him. Can one grow up without the insurance of having been wanted by one's parents?

We then meet Mr Darling: he comes on the scene in 'one of those moods that make him incapable of profiting from domestic bliss'. We discover quite quickly through his words and gestures that he is quite unsure of his authority as a father. That very evening he has a tremendous problem – he cannot tie his cravat! It is of course his wife who must do it for him (as his mother used to?). He looks for her everywhere and is surprised to find her in the nursery with the children, as if he had forgotten about them altogether, and about the fact that he is the father.

Some men have great difficulty in believing that they are a father. One day I received a visit from a young man who was 17 years old, sent to me by his mother who was divorced from the father. The reason for his coming was that despite his evident intelligence he was unable to succeed at school. He was a very agreeable young man and used to come to his sessions on roller skates – his way of 'flying' across the city to see me. We both understood very rapidly that his real reason for coming to see me was to bring me his father. He needed me to convince his father, who was 17 years his senior, of his true role of fatherhood. He constructed his trap very cleverly, and our work ended when his father finally accepted the son under his roof.

Mr Darling is so unsure of his role as a father that he has to create drama around unimportant events in the hope that this will give him the necessary stature:

'I warn you of this, mother, that unless this tie is around my neck we don't go out to dinner tonight, and if I don't go out to dinner tonight, I never go to the office again, and if I don't go to the office again, you and I starve, and our children will be flung into the streets.'

The children are pale with fear as they realize the gravity of the situation.

Mrs Darling knows how to take things in hand; like all good mothers she tries to control the drama that risks destroying her little family: 'Let me try, my dear.'

In a terrible silence their progeny cluster round them. Will she succeed? Their fate depends on it. She fails – no, she succeeds.

In another moment they are wildly gay, romping round the room on each other's shoulders. Father is even a better horse than mother. Michael is dropped upon his bed, Wendy retires to prepare for hers, John runs from Nana, who has reappeared with a bath towel.

Everything appears to be back in order. Nevertheless, Michael seems to have some doubts, as he needs to verify with Mrs Darling that she is his mother, and that she still belongs to him: 'Mother, how did you get to know me?' 'At what time was I born, mother?' 'Oh, mother, I hope I didn't wake you.'

Alas, parents don't perceive the anxiety behind such words; Mrs Darling finds her son cute, and Mr Darling feels the pride of possession: 'Yes, they are cute, aren't they, there is no such thing on earth, and they are ours, ours!'

UNAVOWED FEARS

Even if Mrs Darling is deaf to her son's fears, she does recognize the shadow of her childhood apprehensions of Peter Pan breaking into the nursery. She feels guilty about telling her husband; perhaps she knows that he doesn't like to see her act childishly and would be tempted to take advantage of the situation. She tries nevertheless to share her anxiety with him, but in vain:

> 'Cowardy, cowardy custard.'
> 'No, I am not,' she says, pouting.
> 'Oh yes you are.'
> 'George, I am not.'
> 'Then why not tell?'

She is reassured by such common sense. Sliding her hand into his, with the hope that he will protect them from Peter Pan:

> 'George, what can all this mean?'

It is not easy for parents to maintain their role all the time.

Some, in fact, never even try; when children come along, they consider them as new playmates! They are often known as 'liberal parents'; in fact they are mothers and fathers who have never been able to leave their own childhood behind.

In the Darling family, Mr Darling seems to be one of these 'father children'. Under these circumstances the crucial test to see whether father is solid enough is bound to fail. The children's deception, especially that of Wendy, is inevitable.

It all begins when Michael refuses to take his medicine before going to bed. His father tries reassuring him by telling the story of his own childhood:

> 'When I was your age, Michael, I took medicine without a murmur. I said "Thank you, kind parents, for giving me bottles to make me well." Wendy, who appears in her nightgown, hears this and believes it.
>
> *Wendy*: 'That medicine you sometimes take is much nastier, isn't it, father?'
>
> *Mr Darling* (valuing her support): 'Ever so much nastier. And as an example to you, Michael, I would take it now (thankfully) if I hadn't lost the bottle.'
>
> *Wendy* (always glad to be of service): 'I know where it is, father. I'll fetch it.' She is gone before he can stop her. He turns to John who has come in from the bathroom attired for bed.
>
> *Mr Darling*: 'John, it is the most beastly stuff. It is that sticky sweet kind.'
>
> *John* (who is perhaps still playing at parents): 'Never mind father, it will soon be over.' A spasm of ill-will towards John runs through Mr Darling, and is gone. Wendy returns panting.
>
> *Wendy*: 'Here it is father; I have been as quick as I could.'
>
> *Mr Darling* (with sarcasm that is completely lost on her): 'You have been wonderfully quick, precious quick!' He is now at the foot of Michael's bed, Nana is by its side, holding the medicine spoon insinuatingly in her mouth.
>
> *Wendy* (proudly, as she pours out Mr Darling's medicine): 'Michael, now you will see how father takes it.'
>
> *Mr Darling* (hedging): 'Michael first.'
>
> *Michael* (full of unworthy suspicions): 'Father first.'

Mr Darling: 'It will make me sick, you know.'

John (lightly): 'Come on, father.'

Mr Darling: 'Hold your tongue, sir.'

Wendy (disturbed): 'I thought you took it quite easily, father, saying 'Thank you kind parents, for . . . '

Mr Darling: 'That is not the point, the point is that there is more in my glass than in Michael's spoon. It isn't fair, I swear though it were with my last breath, it is not fair.'

Michael (coldly): 'Father, I'm waiting.'

Mr Darling: 'It's all very well to say you are waiting; so am I waiting.'

Michael: 'Father's a cowardy custard.'

Mr Darling: 'So are you a cowardy custard.' They are now glaring at each other.

Michael: 'I am not frightened.'

Mr Darling: 'Neither am I frightened.'

Michael: 'Well, then, take it.'

Mr Darling: 'Well, then, you take it.'

Wendy (butting in again): 'Why not take it at the same time?'

Mr Darling (haughtily): 'Certainly. Are you ready, Michael?'

Wendy (as nothing has happened): 'One-two-three.' Michael partakes, but Mr Darling resorts to hanky-panky.

John: 'Father hasn't taken his!' Michael howls.

Wendy (pained): 'Oh father!'

Even if the children in this scene seem to have won in terms of power, since it is they and not their father who show parental force and honesty, they have in fact lost everything. Wendy so wanted her father to be a man; faced with such a tarnished paternal image, a bit of her childhood has been lost. Mr Darling feels that he is diminished in his offspring's esteem. Pretending to make a joke, he takes his revenge on Nana, the dog, by making her drink the medication. This just makes things worse and the children take pity on the poor animal. Mr Darling gives way to his jealousy and chases Nana out of the nursery. One would think that Nana is his rival and that in fact he would like to take her place . . .

Mrs Darling, using her maternal intuition, feels that after

such an upsetting incident it would be better not to leave the children alone: 'Oh, how I would like to not go out this evening!' she says with a sigh. Michael, who is so sensitive to his mother's slightest word, starts fretting right away: 'Mother, do you think something can happen to us, even if the night lights are on?'

Mrs Darling prefers to keep her own fears and anxieties quiet at this point: 'No, nothing, my darling. Night lights are mother's eyes that she leaves behind her to protect her children.'

THE ROAD TO NEVER NEVER LAND

Decisive moments in life, those that can turn everything upside down, do not always appear as great adventures. They can present themselves as everyday occurrences that are quickly forgotten. Parents often don't even notice them, even though their children can be transformed by the event.

Mr Darling would never have believed that the little lie concerning the medicine could cost him his children. As he was not very secure in his role as a father, he tried to assert himself by using force unfairly to throw Nana out of the nursery. Unfortunately he was more preoccupied with maintaining his self-image than with being a father capable of keeping his children from tumbling into the Never Never Land.

I think we all have a 'Never Land' somewhere inside us. Some people manage to keep it at a safe distance (with the help of their parents), while others return to it without really knowing why. Describing this internal space is not easy: the Never Never Land is like a map of our minds, with a thousand roads.

Doctors sometimes draw maps of other parts of the body and one's own map can become intensely interesting, but catch them trying to draw a map of a child's mind, which is not only confused, but keeps going around all the time. There are zigzag lines on it, just like temperature on a card, and these are probably roads in the island; for the Never Land is always more or less an island, with astonishing splashes of colour here and there, and coral reefs and rakish-looking craft in the offing, and savages and lonely lairs, and gnomes who are mostly tailors, and caves through which a river runs, and princes with six elder brothers and a hut fast going to decay, and one very small old lady with a hooked nose.

We come at last to meet the captain of the island Never Never Land, who swept me away, just like Wendy, John and Michael, to this place of the spirit where I was able to come close enough to my lost childhood to accept that I should not look for it in reality, but could feel its presence inside.

THE LITTLE STORY THIEF

When we meet him in the nursery, he is a wounded creature who has lost his shadow, but he does not cry for long; he quickly demonstrates how sad children must act, even when they have lost their 'double', the only proof of their material existence. Without a shadow, may we wonder if he is only a reflection of his mother's imagination?

This sad child is so light; he has neither name, nor address, nor mother. One immediately wants to comfort him, but stop! He does not want to be touched!

He ignores what a kiss is. He laughs, he plays with what he does not have and he seems very proud of himself. He is ready to do everything to be admired at all costs, to be respected, to exist at last in the eyes of another person, even if he couldn't in those of his mother.

As we get to know him better, we realize that his good, generous and tender gestures are in fact his way of proving that he exists. The other person is just holding a mirror for him to see himself, and even though she thinks she is indispensable anyone else would do just as well.

Sometimes the mirror is not sufficient proof against the terrible lightness that bears upon the sad child, and he tries other strategies to fill the internal emptiness. That is when he glides into other people's homes, captures the family's heart and feeds on their intimate stories. (Peter wanted the stories that Wendy had heard in her cradle.) He becomes a true pirate, looting other people's treasure.

His great neediness is like a magnet, drawing love and energy to his person and some people, like Wendy, find him particularly touching. They want to repair the tragedy that seems to lurk behind the childish, baby-toothed, smile.

'Boy, why are you crying?,' Wendy asks politely.

Even if the sad child allows himself to cry alone from time to time, he must always be smiling when someone else is looking at him: Peter jumps to his feet, approaches Wendy's bed and offers her a graceful bow, using the way of the fairies. He imitates the fairies very well, but he would so like to be like a real child. He therefore asks Wendy her name: 'Wendy Moira Angela Darling,' she answers. He has only one, very light name – 'Peter Pan' – and an address that doesn't exist: 'Second to the right and straight on until morning'.

When Wendy discovers that Peter Pan has no mother, she realizes that here is a real tragedy. She jumps from her bed and wants to put her arms around Peter, but he is taken aback suddenly. 'No one must ever touch me!' Is he afraid of feeling if one touches him?

Wendy now understands why he was crying a minute ago. Peter denies it of course: 'I was not crying. I can't get my shadow to stick on.'

Peter's shadow is not like that of most other children, because it comes off. One wonders if it really belongs to him, or whether he found it somewhere on his travels. Is it the shadow of a dead child? I think Peter took the shadow to give himself some substance as he is so light.

The proof that he ignores the nature of the shadow is that he thought he could glue it back on simply with soap. Wendy shows him that it has to be sewn on and that it will hurt! She, unlike him, knows her own feelings.

Once the shadow is on, Peter crows like a cock; he is gay and carefree again. Suddenly he seems to need no one and Wendy feels rejected; it is as if she no longer exists for him. He reassures her, the way sad children need reassuring: he flatters her. When a sad child feels a bit lost, it is enough to tell him how wonderful he is, how indispensable he is, for him to perk up immediately.

Peter tries this trick with Wendy: 'Wendy, one girl is of more use than twenty boys!' Wendy wants to give him a kiss all of a sudden. Alas, as with so many intimately human things, a kiss is unknown to Peter. Wendy gives him a button instead. Did she understand that for such essential matters it was best to use such a trick?

The sad children who come to see me often discover that their lives have been filled with fakes for many years. For example, the man who couldn't love a woman; instead it was sports that became the passion of his life, or his work, or a dog. Love for a real woman would be so serious, so full of consequences, that the man prefers to invest his feelings in other things, far from what he really desires. He thus walks on the outside of his life.

Peter is ageless, for he 'escaped on the day he was born'. Wendy is curious about his eternal youth and wants to know the reason: 'It is because I heard my father and mother talking about what I was to be when I became a man. I want always to be a little boy and have fun.' A strange way to tell the story of the sad scene of baby Peter locked out of his mother's window, discovering another child in his cradle!

Nevertheless, Peter knows how to make his tragedy attractive to Wendy. He also knows how to flatter her, and assure her that the lost boys (like himself) are in need of 'female company'. 'Oh Peter, it is splendid the way you talk about girls!'

In fact what interests him especially are the extraordinary fairy tales that she knows. When he discovers that she has even more of them in her head, he becomes almost dangerous – he would like to grab them all from her! 'Come,' he says to her, 'I'll teach you to jump on the wind's back and away we go! Instead of sleeping in your silly bed at night you could be flying with me and saying funny things to the stars. There are mermaids, Wendy, with long tails.' She can hardly remain on the nursery floor. 'Come Wendy, you will see how much we respect you!'

With these last words, Peter touches a sensitive cord. Wendy can resist no longer; she lets herself become light and fly off with him.

THE PROMISED LAND

Canada had always been a 'frontier' land, populated by pioneers, tough people who were prepared to survive in difficult conditions, used to withstanding extremes of nature, climate . . . and emotions. My father, who had grown up under Franz Josef, nourished by Mozart, Thomas Mann and Ady Endre, did not share the same view of life. Furthermore, he had been accustomed to bearing a name known in his country; and he was always surprised when people said of him 'Who is this guy?' Like Peter Pan, landing in Kensington Gardens, he was neither a bird nor a human being in this new world. What would become of him here? I was unable to ask myself that question then.

We found new lodgings on the shores of Lake Ontario in the house of an Irish Catholic woman whose name was Dorothy. The memories of that period remain strongly engraved not only in my mind but also in the family memory.

Years later my mother spoke of the times with 'Dorotja' with great contempt.

It was the beginning of our real life in Canada. There was no time now for dreaming; we had to get organized for survival; we, too, had become 'pioneers'. For my father it was important to find work quickly; for my brother and I, the moment had come to go to school. My mother had to find a way to recreate the family atmosphere.

I shall never forget my first day at school. My father took me in the morning. His warm, firm hands reassured me as we walked the long mile together to Corpus Christi, the local Catholic school. I didn't speak a word of English, but my father was sure that I would learn very quickly.

'Do you think that children here are the same as in Hungary?'

'How will I reply to the teacher?'

'If I have to go to the washroom, how will I say it?'

'Apu, don't leave me, I'm frightened!'

'I shall come to fetch you after school, don't worry, everything will be fine . . .'

There I was in the classroom. The teacher was a very young and pretty nun. Her face, without a trace of makeup, shone with cleanliness and internal warmth. I liked her immediately.

'Hi!' said a girl with a friendly smile. *Haj* (pronounced 'hi') in Hungarian means 'fat, greasy' and I thought of myself as skinny, I didn't understand a thing. At twelve o'clock the bell rang and everyone disappeared in all directions. I did not know that I was to have lunch in the cafeteria, and so I stood waiting for my father at the gate. After a certain time I was the only one left outside the school and I began to get very worried.

Unable to contain myself, I began sobbing desperately; I was lost. A boy from the school, who was walking by, saw my distress and tried to comfort me. I did not understand anything and began to scream in Hungarian at the top of my lungs. No one could decipher the meaning of this strange language. But happily it took me only two weeks to learn to speak English. As a result everyone thought I was a gifted child and allowed me to skip the next class!

In Dorothy's house there were some pleasant moments. Her father, Uncle Bill, liked me; he told me stories and made me toys, and Dorothy used to amuse herself by doing my hair in ways that my mother would never have attempted. It was also in this house that I read my first book, *Tom Sawyer*.

Every evening we would go for a walk, as a family, along the boardwalk on the edge of the lake. At that time the area was considered as run down, as only poor people lived there. Since then all the houses, with their wooden verandahs, have been renovated; property is expensive, and the area is now inhabited by university professors in search of peace and quiet. Dorothy's house is still there, as it was, one of the few that has remained unchanged; it seems so small to me now.

The real drama of that period did not affect me. I would not have understood, although I have the impression that I did feel it. For my parents it was such an enormous shock, that we were never able to talk about it, even later on. As with so many other things that happened to us in Canada, this event was 'buried'; we knew about it, we suffered from it, but we preferred not to recollect it. It became family history.

Dorothy was having sex with my brother! He was hardly 16 years old; he was thin, handsome and very innocent. She was the same age as my mother, but she made herself up, dyed her hair, and seemed much younger than my mother who had aged at least ten years as a result of all our adventures.

A ROOM OF MY OWN

We had to leave Dorothy's very quickly. My father succeeded in finding a brand-new apartment in a middle-class neighbourhood in the west end of Toronto. 'You will have a room of your own. We will paint it sky blue, for an angel,' he told me.

My brother's room was light green. My parents slept in the living room. My father was happy and proud to be able to buy Scandinavian furniture that he liked. We at last had a place of our own, and could forget all the bad adventures.

The fact of having a roof over our heads at last, and redis-covering what it felt to 'exist' again, gave my parents the hope of being able to reconstruct a new life after all. But I also know that my father was disappointed. Canada was certainly not Europe; cultural life was not like in England. He had toyed with the idea of getting Hungarian artists known in Canada by producing Christmas cards with their sketches and paintings. But at the time this kind of art did not correspond either to Canadian tastes nor customs; cards displayed Santa Claus' robust face, with holly sprigs at the four corners; no one was interested in 'naïve' Hungarian paintings!

He soon had to give up his dreams and find other work: first of all at a friend's bank, and then with a Dutch printer. Printing, his real profession, that of the Kanitz family since 1848 – some continuity at last! When I went with him to his office, I loved the smell of paper, ink and pencils; it was just like being back in Hungary.

Sometimes he would come home with some new acquisi-tions, wanting to please and surprise us. One day he brought home an old record player and packages of '45' records, many jazz, and some songs by Bing Crosby and Frank Sinatra. It was true joy to listen and to dance to the music with my father!

I now went to public school. I was just like any little Canadian girl; having adapted to the environment, I felt perfectly at ease. At school I had a best friend, Ruthanne, and in the neighbourhood I had become more or less the leader of my 'gang'. I was a real tomboy and I owed my reputation to all the stories I invented. Sometimes we were on an island populated by 'lost boys' and pirates . . . I was Peter Pan, of course!

THE CRAB

I don't know exactly how it all happened, but immediately I realized how serious the situation was. One morning my father got up looking very pale. My mother insisted that he see a doctor immediately, but before he could go out, he fainted on the doorstep. He had vomited blood during the night.

Memory is strange. It seems to me that my recollection of this moment stops, becomes confused . . . in any case, my father was hospitalized. They thought it was an ulcer, but the fatal word was pronounced very quickly: 'Cancer . . . cancer of the spine'. In Hungarian the word was *rak*, the crab: it all seemed very mysterious to me. What could it be doing inside my father's body? Yet the possibility had already crossed my mind, because he had been anxious that something was eating him from inside.

It is only later that the effects of a tragedy emerge in a sad child. There is no way of knowing how the sad child will react to a drama, and how she will make it her own. Nevertheless, these very personal strategies make us what we are. When I listen to an individual's story I always marvel at the unique, creative techniques he uses to cope with life.

Even as I was completely helpless when confronted with the calamity that was to take away my childhood forever, something sparked off premature feelings and emotions in me. After the shock of our departure from Hungary, the present circumstances precipitated the moment for my leaving the nursery; like Wendy, I needed to see my father as a man. Suddenly, he interested me in a different way; everything about him fascinated me.

'Mummy, is father a Jew?' I thought about his nose; it

wasn't 'hooked', but a little turned down. I had been told that Jews had hooked noses. We were reading *Oliver Twist* at school; the figure of Fagin was a caricature. I liked my father's bald head. It shone at the top and I used to give it a little kiss as I passed by when he was reading in the armchair. I liked his hands. They were slim and neat, with hairs growing at the knuckles. I liked his hairs, and when he took me to the movies I would put my hand on his arm and twirl his hairs into little knots. Sometimes he would lie down on my bed to read me stories. One day, when he was reading *Robinson Crusoe* and I was lying close to him, I felt a strange electrical impulse going through my body.

The Toronto General Hospital was downtown, and the trip was long and interesting. As one approached the centre of the city, the houses became older, and then gave way to big buildings. It must have reminded me a little of Budapest – I was constantly looking for a smell, a colour, a stone, a street corner from the past.

The hospital was enormous. My mother, although usually without any sense of direction, succeeded in finding the room. I was overwhelmed by the stink of the place and the rows of white beds. I felt a kind of disagreeable nausea rising from my stomach and blocking my throat. Suddenly I was very frightened.

Towards the middle of the large hall, we could identify my father. He was much thinner and he smiled weakly. They had conducted some very painful tests on him, including a coloured injection into the spine. A man was sitting on his bed, a colleague from work. 'Yes, there is a tumour and they must operate. Probably cancerous. I thought that it was only rheumatism. Do you remember how in Austria the toes on my left foot became numb?'

'Yes, I remember,' said my mother, in a disbelieving tone. 'Cancer! It is not possible, it is not possible!'

'But you know, a very good doctor is dealing with me. The Canadians are very advanced in this kind of surgery.

Everything will be alright, you will see!' Nothing bad could happen in the 'Promised Land' – there are no bad surprises in the Never Never Land, only adventures!

The tests results came a few days later and were positive, and my father was operated on immediately. The operation lasted ten hours, and they removed a cancerous tumour from his spine. I can't really remember the days that followed the operation. He was very weak and thin when he was able to come home at last.

A LITTLE MOTHER FOR APU

After his return we made some changes to our apartment, and to our lives. My brother stopped school and became a worker in a large baking factory. The bread was made on a production line; it was white and soft like cotton, and we hated it because we came from a country where bread was brown and had taste. The work was hard; my brother worked night shifts and his arms became strong and muscular. He only thought about one thing: he wanted to buy a Pontiac car so that he could realize the dream that he and my father had created on the boat coming over: 'In Canada we will become rich, we will ride in an American car and visit Niagara Falls!'

My mother was very surprised when my father agreed to let my brother stop school at 16. She thought that his illness must have made him weak. Later on, I understood that other things also came into the way of him being a father to his son. One image comes to my mind of that period: my brother rolling on the ground in a rage and my father just watching him, looking sad and shattered. That day I locked myself into the bathroom to pray to God that my brother would go crazy!

My father must have returned home during the school holidays because I remember staying with him for long hours, while my mother worked. I made him fried eggs, I cleaned the house, I played at being a 'little mother' for him.

But especially I sat for hours at his bedside and we talked about everything together.

'Apu, tell me about when you were a little boy. What did you like, what did you play with, what did you wear?'

'Apu, how did you meet Anju? Was she beautiful? Did you love her?'

'And when you were a soldier on a horse? And when you were a prisoner?'

'Apu, do you think that God exists?'

'Apu, tell me everything you know.'

'Apuka, tell-me, tell-me, tell-me!'

He never tired of telling me stories about his childhood; how at the age of six he got up at midnight and crossed the cemetery that was near their house to prove to himself that he was not afraid. He told me about the war, Russia, and how he met my mother. I loved these moments of 'stories' and how he was determined to nourish me with all of it. It was as if he felt the urgency. He wanted to tell me everything all at once, things that take a lifetime to tell . . . everything? I was only ten, and I especially retained the images, the colours, the vibrations. My father told me other things as well, but the words got lost; or perhaps I didn't understand them.

At other moments, when my father was tired, and I wasn't playing at being 'little mother', I simply stayed in my room. It was at one of these moments that by mistake I let the inkwell drop and the dark-blue liquid made nasty spots on the sky-blue wall. I must have cried out, because my father woke up, ran into my room and began slapping me so violently that he couldn't stop. I was so staggered that I couldn't even cry; I had turned into stone. When my father finally came to his senses, he collapsed and we both cried desperately.

THE CRAB TAKES OVER

After a short respite during which he was able to take on a seemingly normal life, the pain returned. He started to limp and had to go back to hospital. This time they gave him radiotherapy without any tests to identify the cancer. When the pain became unbearable they operated again, only to discover that the 'crab' had taken over his whole body.

Once again, my father came home in an ambulance. He was weaker than before. I don't know why, but this time I didn't play the 'little mother'; I think my mother stayed with him, while I played from morning till night with my 'gang'. I vaguely remember my father saying: 'You are letting me down, this time . . .'

I must have created a distance to protect myself. In fact I don't even remember whether he started working again after this operation. But soon he was hospitalized at St Michael's hospital. My mother and I went to see him regularly, and spent Saturdays and Sundays with him. I still remember all the details of his room; I also recall the depressed faces of the other patients as we walked past them to reach room number 53. My father grew very thin, but he still smiled and never complained.

'You know,' he said to my mother, 'I should have taken greater advantage of my life with you. I should have married you earlier! You are the love of my life . . .' One day he seemed especially happy when we arrived, as if he had found the solution to an important problem.

'Today I spoke to the social worker about Kati's future. She promised that she would assist with her university education.' We never saw the social worker again, but the important thing was that she had been able to give hope to my father. I became passionately devoted to my father's desire; to go to university became the main objective of my life.

On Saturdays my mother and I would go to the cinema before visiting my father in hospital. We would take sandwiches, and if the film was good we would watch it a second time around. This is how we saw *Gone with the Wind*; I was very moved by the film, and must have seen it at least 30 times since. At the end I was crying so desperately that my mother had to shake me: 'Kati, Kati, it's only a film, it's only a film!'

Once, after one of these sessions, I tried to fix my hair to look like Scarlett O'Hara, thinking I would please my father. I started to envisage myself becoming a woman, and needed my father to survive the test.

When mothers and fathers are steadfast in their parental role so as to assist their children at the difficult moment of leaving the nursery, they unknowingly support them when they face important decisions such as choosing their sex. Just as at birth, when the question of 'boy' or 'girl' is such a determining factor, it is fundamental at this point to under stand the difference between 'woman' or 'man'. Without the presence of parents and their calming support, the problem of 'sex' can become enormously difficult for the child.

This feeling of having to choose can discourage the sad child from wanting to grow up. If Peter Pan left his home on the day of his birth, it is because he wanted to keep the two choices, between boy and girl. At the end of the story, he cannot bear the fact that Wendy has chosen to become a 'woman'.

My first efforts to leave the nursery were hindered by difficult circumstances. My parents were in a weakened state, and even if I tried to hang on to the memories of my father and his desires for my future, in reality his hands were letting me go, little by little. I therefore turned to my mother and clung to her more and more, rediscovering the very begin-ning of life. I was like Peter Pan, returning to the window, and my mother let me in, for she also needed to hang on to her daughter, as she would have done with her own mother in such extreme circumstances. I therefore put off the choice of 'sex' for another day, even though I was very curious to know the truth about 'men and women'.

One day a panic-stricken friend in my class told me that her mother was bleeding when she went to the toilet. It frightened me as well, and that evening, as my mother was preparing dinner, I sat in the chair next to the window and told her what was happening to Valerie's mother. 'Do you think she will die? She must be losing all her blood!' My mother started laughing, despite herself. 'It is not an illness, you know, it is quite natural, all women have it. When you grow up you too will bleed every month.'

I was horrified and started to cry. I felt that I had lost something irretrievable; but at the same time an immense curiosity was born in me.

THE LAST VISIT

After my father's second operation, we rearranged the apartment once again. My brother slept in my blue room, and my mother and I occupied the room that my parents had shared since the illness. I slept in my father's place; I hold very special memories of that bed.

'Tell me, Anjuka, what men and women do?'

'It is very pleasant . . . but *what* is so pleasant?'

'Yes, but with all that I still don't understand how a child can look like his father!'

My mother explained every night. She never got tired of my questions; she didn't mind talking to me about it all. At last I understood, but at the same time I did not *really* understand.

It was in my father's bed that I had my first menstruation; it was in my father's bed that I cried over his death.

It was the beginning of spring. The hospital had a park where I would play from time to time when the afternoons became too long in the cancer ward. This particular time my mother sent me to the park and I started picking a bunch of violets for him: 'If I pray very hard, God will surely help him to get well . . .'

My father could no longer speak. His yellowed skin stuck to his cheekbones, and his tongue seemed so thick that the words had become impossible. He signalled for us to come and kiss him. He was very hot and agitated, as if he saw something that was beyond his grasp. He made signs of blessing with his hands, the only part of his body that remained unchanged, and that were still so familiar to me. . . My mother sent me to the garden. I kissed my father's hand, without knowing that it would be the last time.

My brother was in a hurry as usual, and wanted to take us home before his next rendezvous. We left in a rush; I didn't get the chance to give my father the bouquet of violets. My mother was crying. When we arrived home we got a telephone call from the hospital: 'Your husband has just passed away.'

Two days later I answered the phone to a man who knew my father: 'No, he is not here, he is dead.' The man asked to speak to my mother. He congratulated her on having such a brave daughter.

For the funeral ceremony we chose the Hungarian church in the immigrant district of Toronto. First we had to go to the funeral home where the dead are at rest among the flowers. I found the odour was worse than that of the hospital. My father's face was transformed; they had blown it up with some fluid, and had put rouge and lipstick on to make him look better. The only thing I recognized about him were his hands, still fine and beautiful, hands that had been so warm. It was only in the church when they closed the coffin and the organs began to play that I started screaming with pain and rage. 'Apu, Apu, don't leave me, don't leave me alone, I am frightened!'

We buried him in the new part of a Canadian cemetery, near where we were living. There were no trees; only the hole in the ground seemed to break the monotony of the land. We had no money to buy a gravestone, so my mother, brother and I made a wooden cross out of mahogany; we varnished it with several layers so that it would be strong. The cemetery did not allow us to put it up because only stones were permitted, so my father's tomb remained unmarked, except for a small corner where his adopted name was written. At first I used to go and see him on my bike. Then we moved, and the journey became too long for me to cycle . . .

3

The Past, the Passage and the Passer

It seems that the borders of the past always remain hazy. We think we have closed the door and changed our identity, never to look back again, and yet if the passage has not been completed, the past continues to hover over us like a ghost.

The border from Hungary to Austria, which we crossed on that famous night in 1949, seemed very disappointing to me, since there was no obvious 'passage' from one state to another. It is also possible that at that time I wasn't mature enough for such a transition, and perhaps this is why it left me so disoriented.

Obviously this is one of the reasons why, when I finally became old enough to have a passport and to travel, I never stopped crossing borders: Toronto . . . Quebec . . . Paris . . . London . . . Geneva . . . Paris . . . Bombay . . . Nairobi . . . Rio . . . Tokyo . . . Sao-Paolo . . . New York . . . Stockholm . . . Rome . . . Paris . . . I always settled in temporarily; as soon as I started to put down roots, something told me that it was time to move on. So I had to go on, once again, to cross the border, make the passage, begin again.

A NAME TO HIDE BEHIND

My father also thought that he could always begin again; history had provided him with many reasons to try. During World War II, he had been appalled and horrified when those very same Hungarians who had knighted his Jewish family (who originated from Moravia 400 years earlier) had forced them to wear the yellow star. The Kanitz Printing Company had served its country for several generations, and all of a sudden its owners were being slaughtered. Having barely escaped from the hands of those persecutors, he nearly fell into those of another. The uniform and the style was different; instead of Hitler, the newcomer was called Stalin: one assassin had replaced the other.

Once again, we tried to hide. This time, it wasn't in the cupboards or cellars; it was a different kind of hiding, behind a new name. But we didn't realize that in this new hiding place we would no longer know who we were; we had hidden from ourselves.

Border crossings are fundamental steps in the life of a human being; we go from one stage to another, so giving up events that gave us such great pleasure in the past. These are always trying times; all cultures and religions have invented rites of passage, not only to make the voyage easier, but also to make sure that there is no possible return. There is always the temptation to go back to the original nest, the mother's womb. This cannot be done without a passer, a guide, often an exceptional person who has directly experienced this ordeal and who has been granted the legal right to bring others across.

The sad child is the one who has not been able to pass: 'All, children, except one, grow up . . .' – the sad child. For him or her, the passages have not been made, or have been made badly, or the guide was not the right one. Or the child passes too early or too late. During such a passage, the sad child loses an essential part of himself or herself, and is forever looking back to try to find it again; he or she is not free to grow up. Escape, flight, cannot offer passages from one state to another, and hence any possibility of starting anew is precluded.

Without passports, bearing a name that was not our own, with illegal passage guides, we set out for the New World. Thus, without knowing it, we were losing much more than our house on Lake Balaton, our Budapest apartment, and our Kanitz Printing Company; we were losing ourselves. I was small, I looked back, I saw my rabbit disappear, and I carried away in my heart the Never Never Land of my childhood. As for my father, there was no way that he could have survived this passage.

When the passage isn't successfully achieved, when the differences are unclear, the past permeates the present, and the future begins to resemble the past. The genders and the generations merge: parents are no longer parents, boys and girls become the same, and children play at being the parents of their own parents.

The only alternative in a situation of this kind is: for or against . . . kill or be killed . . . eat or be eaten. Life loses all its complexity, and the nuances are no longer perceptible. This extreme simplification should remind us of our origins, the 'very beginning' when nothing existed outside 'mother' and 'not mother', her vital presence or her absence.

Peter Pan's Never Never Land bore a strange resemblance to all this. The question remains: was the passage of Wendy, John and Michael to the Never Land truly a passage to growing up, or was it just another adventure of no importance? Was it a step forward, or a big somersault backwards? I am inclined to favour the somersault, even though it had no tragic consequences for Wendy (as for her brothers, we do not know).

Peter Pan did not have the traits of a traveller. He was a sad child, deeply wounded, who sought refuge in the Never Land because he could not do anything else. He brought the

Darling children along with him, but not to allow them to grow up (which is often the case in other fairy tales). Besides, he was such an inattentive guardian that he nearly lost them on the way. If he had decided to take them along, it was only because of his own personal needs, to take from them what he most lacked: a mother.

ON THE WINGS OF THE WIND

Those who claim not to know the Never Never Land are mistaken, because we have all been there some time or other, even if only fleetingly.

It is true that in growing up we watch the little island of our childhood recede into the distance, become misty and pale, and we might imagine it going out like a waning candle. But sometimes it only takes an odour, a ray of sun dancing on a white wall, a note of music, or a simple street corner, for the Never Land to reappear, and for us to be catapulted backwards to where time does not exist.

When this happens everything becomes possible again. We are at once air and breather, water and drinker, king and queen, boy and girl. We can be both here and there at the same time. We can speak or say nothing, because we are always understood. In one instant, we can transform ourselves into someone else: father, mother, brother or sister; we are all equal. And the master of the island must always be at the centre.

In the daytime, we can live through many experiences in the Never Land and emerge from each one a hero. But at nightfall the landscape of the island suddenly assumes new contours. Familiar objects appear strange, wild animals spring from their lairs. The queen turns into a huge tentacular spider. Father and mother disappear, and we are suddenly tiny and defenceless. Some people have seen the Never Land at night, and prefer to forget it. Others return there with great pleasure, to rediscover the child they left behind, without whose memory it would be difficult to continue living.

'Second to the right, and then straight on till morning.'

That, Peter had told Wendy, was the way to the Never Land; but even birds, carrying maps and consulting them at windy corners, could not have sighted it with these instructions. Peter just said anything that came into his head.

At first his companions trusted him implicitly, and so great were the delights of flying that they wasted time circling round church spires or any other tall objects on the way that took their fancy . . . Sometimes it was dark, and sometimes light, and now they were very cold and again too warm. Did they really feel hungry at times, or were they merely pretending because Peter had such a jolly new way of feeding them? His way was to pursue birds who had food in their mouths suitable for humans and snatch it from them. But Wendy noticed with gentle concern that Peter did not seem to know that this was rather an odd way of getting your bread and butter, nor even that there are other ways.

There were certainly many things that Peter did not know, and this was surely why he had insisted on taking Wendy and her brothers to the Never Land. His visits to the window of No 14 enabled him to see how real children act when they have a mother all to themselves, who watches them growing up. It is difficult to grow up unless a mother is watching over you.

What could Wendy teach Peter? Did he simply want her to look at him through a mother's eyes? On the way, he never stopped 'grandstanding'; for instance, 'Peter would fly close to the water and touch each shark's tail in passing . . . (the children) could not follow him in this with much success, so perhaps it was rather like showing off, especially as he kept looking behind', to make sure that he was being duly admired.

TRAPS OF MEMORY

Sometimes he left them alone. This enabled him 'to have an adventure in which they had no share. He would come down laughing over something fearfully funny he had been saying to a star, but he had already forgotten what it was, or he would come up with mermaid scales still sticking to him and yet not be able to say for certain what had been happening. It was rather irritating to children who had never seen a mermaid.

'And if he forgets them so quickly,' Wendy argued, 'how can we expect that he will go on remembering us?'

Indeed, sometimes when he returned he did not remember them, at least not well. Wendy was sure of it. She saw recognition come into his eyes as he was about to pass them the time of day and go on; once she even had to tell him her name.

'I'm Wendy,' she said agitatedly.

He was very sorry. 'I say, Wendy,' he whispered to her 'always if you see me forgetting you, just keep on saying "I'm Wendy", and then I'll remember.'

Of course, this was rather unsatisfactory. However, to make amends he showed them how to lie out flat on a strong wind that was going their way, and this was such a pleasant change that they tried it several times and found they could sleep thus with security. Indeed they would have slept longer, but Peter tired quickly of sleeping, and soon he would cry in his captain's voice, 'We get off here.'

Peter's lapses of memory are an indication of his deep sadness and of his inability to truly connect with anyone.

The children interest him because he believes he can feed on their substance as 'real children'. But as soon as his attention is diverted by something else, it is as if he were totally unaware of their existence.

Curiously, the Never Land was not unknown to the Darling children:' "Wendy, look at the turtles, burying their eggs in the sand." "I say, John, I see your flamingo with the broken leg." "Look, Michael, there's your cave." Peter was a little annoyed with them for knowing so much.' Yet the time came when the Never Land began to look dark and threatening.

> Then unexplored patches arose in it and spread; black shadows moved about in them; the roar of the beasts of prey was quite different now, and above all, you lost the certainty that you would win. You were quite glad that the night-lights were on. You even liked Nana to say that this was just the mantelpiece over here and that Neverland was all make-believe . . . but it was real now, and there were no night-lights, and it was getting darker every moment, and where was Nana?

Deprived of his mother's attention, Peter had to face the Never Land alone. This is why the terrible side might emerge at any moment, and yet this did not appear to concern him unduly.

For example, death did not concern him: 'There's a pirate asleep in the pampas just beneath us,' he explained to John. 'If you like, we'll go down and kill him.'

Peter tried to make the children believe that killing a pirate was no more serious than having a cup of tea, and he promised that they would have great adventures. When they discovered that the pirate captain was none other than the terrible 'Captain Hook' and that Peter had cut off Hook's right hand to feed the crocodile, the children could easily imagine the scale of terror which reigned over the island.

Peter remained unperturbed when John whispered huskily in fear: 'He has an iron hook instead of a right hand, and he claws with it?' 'Exactly.'

CAPTAIN SAD

Kill or be killed. That's the basic rule on the island, but there is another fundamental rule which everyone has to obey: it is prohibited to grow up and to say the word 'mother'.

The two captains of the island are, naturally, Peter Pan,

the leader of the Lost Boys, and Captain Hook, the chief of the pirates. Are they not one and the same person?

Hook is the saddest of the sad children, whereas Peter Pan is young, gay and heartless; Hook is old and sinister, but also heartless. Since Peter cut off Hook's hand and fed it to the crocodile, his situation has worsened. He already had a very bad self-image, but this amputation wounded his soul as much as his body.

Hook speaks in a manner of a man educated in the best British schools. Like Mr Darling, he is extremely touchy about what people think of him. What he finds most unbearable in Peter Pan is his self-assurance, something that he himself has lost and wants so much to recapture.

Let us take a closer look at him. 'He lay at his ease in a rough chariot, drawn and propelled by his men, and instead of a right hand he had the iron hook with which ever and anon he encouraged them to increase their pace. As dogs this terrible man treated and addressed them, and as dogs they obeyed him. In person he was cadaverous and dark-skinned, and his hair was dressed in long curls, which at a distance looked like black candles and made him look particularly threatening. His eyes were as blue as forget-me-nots, but profoundly melancholy, save when he was plunging his hook into you, when two red spots appeared and lit them up horribly.

> In manner, something aristocratic still clung to him. He could be extremely charming, and I have been told that he was a raconteur of repute. He was never more sinister than when he was most polite, which is probably the truest test of breeding; and the elegance of his diction, even when he was swearing, no less than the distinction of his demeanour, showed him one of a different cast from his crew.
>
> A man of indomitable courage, it was said of him that the only thing he shied at was the sight of his own blood, which was thick and of an unusual colour. . . . Such is the terrible man against whom Peter Pan is pitted. Who will win?

The sad child sometimes has a father Hook. This father, himself profoundly sad, digs his hook into his son, and clutches at the young image of himself, offering him the picture of a wounded and passive creature. The sad child is thus prevented from living his own life, and cannot but identify with a paternal image that is wounded and sick, and is doomed to transmit this image in turn.

An athletic young man suffering from violent stomach pains came to see me. After dismissing any medical reasons, his pain obviously stemmed from something else. He could not understand the cause of his suffering because he led an ordinary, uneventful existence, yet this problem prevented him from enjoying the pleasures of life: his academic success, music and dance. He frequented women little, and only allowed himself affairs with those who were already attached. From time to time he tried to end his suffering through dangerous sports in which he risked his life, but this never worked. By the time he had achieved success, he'd already lost any pleasure in the activity. At our first session he talked about his difficult relationship with his father, a quiet man discontented with life, who had never played with him. At the age of five, he received a train for Christmas and didn't want to open the package, hoping that his father would play with him. But his father remained as passive as ever, and the little boy never took the train out of its box.

One day the image of this father emerged: he was sad, alone, smoking a cigarette, and waiting to resume the work he hated. This pathetic image returned and burrowed into him like a hook: 'He's the one who prevents me from living, the bastard,' the young man cried out on discovering this tormented father in the pit of his stomach. After that, the battle was long and the question, 'Which one will win?' weighed heavily throughout our work.

BECAUSE OF THE CROCODILE

For some sad children, the strategy pursued by Peter Pan – in other words to be gay, innocent and heartless – is not easy to adopt, because the crocodile is always scary. I have known some of these children: as soon as they feel better and start to laugh again, the crocodile reappears to persecute them. The next day, they are sadder than before.

One possible alternative for them is to raise a dog or a wild animal. The crocodile then remains outside and cannot get inside the person. The dog or wild animal tends to bite others, and be faithful and gentle to his master. Once when I was bitten by a friend's dog, she said to me, apologetically: 'He only bites people I like!'

Captain Hook did not have a moment of peace between Peter Pan, who pursued him, and the crocodile, who fought him everywhere. So confrontation was inevitable, and the opportunity was provided by the capture of Peter's friend Tiger Lily, the little Indian girl: two of Hook's men captured Lily and dragged her, solidly bound with cords, into their boat. They were ordered to abandon her on Marooner's Rock, to be drowned when the tide rose.

> Quite near the rock, but out of sight, two heads were bobbing up and down, Peter's and Wendy's. Wendy was crying, for it was the first tragedy she had seen. Peter had seen many tragedies, but he had forgotten them all. He was less sorry than Wendy for Tiger Lily: it was two against one that angered him, and he meant to save her.
>
> An easy way would have been to wait until the pirates had gone, but he was never one to choose the easy way.

Clearly, it is easier to defend principles than it is to experience feelings! He therefore decided to imitate Hook's voice and order the pirates to release Tiger Lily. This worked like a charm, because something he loved to do, and always did best, was to imitate someone else. Was he beginning to slide into Hook's skin?

In any case, the pirates obeyed and cut Tiger Lily's cords, at the very moment when the real Hook swam to the boat.

In the light of the lantern Wendy saw his hook grip the boat's side; she saw his evil swarthy face as he rose dripping from the water. 'The game's up, . . . those boys have found a mother. '

Hook can only pursue his evil schemes in the absence of a 'mother'.

IDENTITY

But Peter did not enjoy the success of his ruse for long, because the pirate captain began to suspect something:

'Spirit that haunts the dark lagoon tonight,' he cried, 'dost hear me?' Of course Peter should have kept quiet, but he did not. He immediately answered in Hook's voice:
'Odds, bobs, hammer and tongs, I hear you.'
In that supreme moment Hook did not blanch, even at the gills, but Smee and Starky clung to each other in terror.
'Who are you stranger, speak?' Hook demanded.
'I am James Hook,' replied the voice, 'Captain of the *Jolly Roger.*'
'You are not,' Hook cried hoarsely.
Hook tried a more ingratiating manner. 'If you are Hook,' he said almost humbly, 'come tell me, who am I?'
'A codfish,' replied the voice, 'only a codfish.'
'A codfish!' Hook echoed blankly.
And it was then, but not till then, that his proud spirit broke. He saw his men draw back from him.
'Have we been captained all this time by a codfish!' they muttered. 'It is lowering to our pride.'
But . . . he scarcely heeded them. Against such fearful evidence it was not their belief in him that he needed, it was his own. He felt his ego slipping from him. 'Don't desert me, bully,' he whispered hoarsely to it.
In his dark nature there was a touch of the feminine, as in all

the great pirates, and it sometimes gave him intuitions. Suddenly he tried the guessing game.

'Hook,' he called, 'have you another voice?'

Now Peter could never resist a game, and he answered blithely in his own voice, 'I have.'

'And another name?'

'Aye, aye.'

'Vegetable?' asked Hook.

'No.'

'Mineral?'

'No.'

'Animal?'

'Yes.'

'Man?'

'No!' This answer rang out scornfully.

'Boy?'

'Yes.'

'Ordinary boy?'

'No!'

'Wonderful boy?'

To Wendy's pain the answer that rang out this time was 'Yes . . . Can't guess?' crowed Peter. 'Do you give up?'

Of course in his pride he was carrying the game too far, and the miscreants saw their chance.

'Yes, yes,' they answered eagerly.

'Well, then,' he cried, 'I am Peter Pan.'

'Pan!'

This declaration changed everything for Hook. Strange to say, he had both to destroy and preserve the image of the wonderful boy, so that he himself could be something other than a poor codfish. A father Hook needs the presence of his son, the only justification for a pleasureless life, in order to transmit his wound.

PAINFUL INJUSTICE

Henceforth, the confrontation was inevitable.

It was not in the water that they met. Hook rose to the rock to breathe, and at the same moment Peter scaled it on the opposite side. The rock was slippery as a ball, and they had to crawl rather than climb. Neither knew that the other was coming. Each feeling for a grip met the other's arm: in surprise they raised their heads; their faces were almost touching.

One would have thought that Peter would be afraid at this moment.

But Peter had one feeling only, gladness. And he gnashed his pretty teeth with joy. Quick as thought he snatched a knife from Hook's belt and was about to drive it home, when he saw that he was higher up the rock than his foe. It would not have been fighting fair. He gave the pirate a hand to help him up.

It was then that Hook bit him.

Not the pain of this but its unfairness was what dazed Peter. It made him quite helpless. He could only stare, horrified. Every child is affected thus the first time he is treated unfairly. All he thinks he has a right to when he comes to you to be yours is fairness. After you have been unfair to him he will love you again, but he will never afterwards be quite the same boy. No one ever gets over the first unfairness; no one except Peter. He often met it, but he always forgot it. I suppose that was the real difference between him and all the rest.

So when he met it now it was like the first time; and he could just stare, helpless. Twice the iron hand clawed him.'

Peter, wounded, remained alone on the rock which 'was very small now; soon it would be submerged. Pale rays of light tiptoed across the waters; and by and by there was to be heard a sound at once the most musical and the most melancholy in the world: the mermaids calling to the moon.

Peter was not quite like other boys; but he was afraid at last. A tremor ran through him, like a shudder passing over the sea; but on the sea one shudder follows another till there are hundreds of them, and Peter felt just the one. Next moment he was standing erect on the rock again, with that smile on his face and a drum beating within him. It was saying, 'to die will be an awfully big adventure.'

'To die will be an awfully big adventure': these words distinguish Peter from the other children and they betray the depth of his sadness. When the inability to feel is powerful enough to extinguish even the fear of death, it means that the child can go no further in desolation and despair. Since he is capable of playing with what he does not have, his very life becomes the challenge of a great adventure.

PRETENDING

Everything was play in the Never Land. But the favourite game of the lost boys and the Darling children, since they arrived in the island, was 'fathers and mothers'. Wendy acted the 'little mother' to perfection, and Peter obviously took the role of 'father'. One day, this game, so close to reality, disturbed him; he was 'not sure' whether he was awake or asleep.

> 'Peter, what is it?'
> 'I was just thinking,' he said, a little scared. 'It is only make-believe, isn't it, that I am their father?'
> 'Oh, yes,' Wendy said primly . . . 'Peter,' she asked, trying to speak firmly, 'what are your exact feelings for me?'
> 'Those of a devoted son, Wendy.'
> 'I thought so, she said, and went and sat by herself at the extreme end of the room.'

Peter was perfectly sincere; he was incapable of imagining what a women could expect of him, except to protect him by creating a very comfortable base for him.

Is it possible for a man to love a woman when he lives with his father's hook in the pit of his stomach? Like Peter, this son tends to be passive towards a woman, to treat her like a mother, because if he permitted himself to desire her sexually he would be afraid of killing her. Sexual desire is a blend of aggressiveness and tenderness; when tenderness is paralysed, aggressiveness becomes murderous.

As time passes, sad children realize that it is no longer possible to 'pretend' by playing 'fathers and mothers'; that a love story between a man and a woman is a very serious matter, and that it can hurt.

One day a man came to tell me his story. Listening to him, I was struck by the idea that this man had never experienced love with a woman, despite two marriages and many affairs. Though I am not in the habit of asking intimate questions directly, I suddenly said: 'Have you ever loved a woman?' He gazed at me somewhat surprised, reflected and then answered: 'No, never.'

Few men and women succeed in being honest with each other on these questions. Yet sad children, when they find themselves marooned in an adult's body, often come to ask for advice. Because even if they can easily pretend, things are different for their partners.

Sometimes the man, Peter Pan, finds a Wendy ready to accept everything, but also very often, when Wendy is tired and leaves her Peter, he just stays there, completely lost, having understood nothing of what happened.

Was it the disappointment in a man, as previously with her father, which made Wendy decide to leave the Never Land for ever? In any case, she felt that there was no short-cut to growing up; pretending to be a mother would not help her to become one. Sometimes women who have not yet fulfilled their childhood decide to have a child, in the hope that this will make them grow up. Alas, the baby placed in this situation is liable to respond to the deep needs of its mother, in other words to play the maternal role, thus renouncing his crib from the day he is born.

Wendy realized that she still needed her true mother to be able to become a mother in turn. This thought was accompanied by a new awareness: her mother might be anxious about her absence. For the first time she agreed to experience her mother's feelings. Was this a step towards motherhood?

All this was possible for Wendy because she 'knew how the love of a mother is infinite'. Unlike Peter, she was convinced that her mother had left the window open for her children to return. She repeated this confidently in the story that she told the children every night.

But she violated the rules of the Never Land. By allowing her true mother to enter (a way of accepting her origins), she also introduced time – in other words, the future.

THE EYES OF A MOTHER

'Did they ever go back?' asked one of the lost boys.

'Let's now,' said Wendy, 'take a peep into the future.'

'Years have rolled by. . . . See, dear brothers,' says Wendy, pointing upwards, 'there is the window still standing open. Ah, now we are rewarded for our sublime faith in a mother's love.' So up they flew to their mummy and daddy, and pen cannot describe the happy scene, over which we draw a veil.

But Peter was so disturbed by this story that he decided to unveil his secret, the tragedy of his life:

'Long ago,' he said, 'I thought like you that my mother would always keep the window open for me; so I stayed away for moons and moons and moons, and then flew back; but the window was barred, for mother had forgotten all about me, and there was another little boy sleeping in my bed.'

'Wendy, let's go home,' cried John and Michael together.

So you can see that the decision to leave the Never Land can be taken very quickly, once the right time has come. Wendy was ready to bring everyone back to real life, where mothers are mothers and children are children . . . but Peter refused to follow them.

To show that their departure would leave him unmoved, he skipped up and down the room, playing gaily on his heartless pipes.

'To find your mother,' she coaxed.

Now, if Peter had ever quite had a mother, he no longer missed her. He could do very well without one. He had thought them out, and remembered only their bad points.

A sad child said to me one day: 'I miss my mother terribly', and I felt that nothing more horrible could happen to her. Often, the sad child can only express his/her bad feelings about the mother. Like the young woman who came to see me over a number of years, telling me how horrible her mother had been to her. The most 'horrible' thing was that her mother had left her daughter with her grandmother for some time when she was only three. But the daughter could not really feel that wound; so instead she invented a witch of a mother, on whom she could spit her venom. When she had sorted it out her mother became a wonderful and loving woman again.

Nothing and no one in the world could persuade Peter to leave the Never Land, because he clung so strongly to the negative image of his mother. It was his most precious possession.

One sometimes feels that the child can detach himself more easily when the image of the mother is so negative. Often, the very opposite occurs, and the child never succeeds in getting away. The man who could not love any woman said one day that he felt the presence of his mother everywhere. Although she had been dead for years, he had the impression that she was lurking behind every door. A mother like this can only bar the road to love, because her son must gather up all his strength to resist her.

DEPARTURE FROM THE NEVER LAND

The Never Land is never dismantled easily; it never vanishes without a fight! Though Peter didn't want to follow the children, he pretended to help them in their plans for departure; this moment of inattention enabled Hook to achieve his sinister plan. Taking advantage of the fact that no one was thinking about the pirates, he succeeded in capturing the children and dragging them to his ship! In the Never Land one can never be sure of anything; the most terrible conflicts can break out in a single instant of distraction, especially if a change is taking place.

When Peter Pan learned of the capture of Wendy and the lost boys, he swore to rescue them and took a terrible oath: 'Hook or me this time.'

Captain Hook paced the deck unsteadily. Despite his apparent triumph, there was no elation in his step; he was profoundly dejected.

> He was often thus when communing with himself on board ship in the quietude of the night. It was because he was so terribly alone. This inscrutable man never felt more alone than when surrounded by his dogs.

Peter, determined to rule the Never Land, found the way to get everything back to normal. Once again, he resorted to his strategy of imitation: he slid into the skin of the crocodile. He had seen the crocodile pass by without noticing anything peculiar about it, but then he remembered that it had not been ticking . . .

> Without giving a thought to what might be the feelings of a fellow creature thus abruptly deprived of its closest companion, Peter at once considered how he could turn the catastrophe to his own use; and he decided to tick . . . and ticked superbly.

With this new identity, he climbed aboard the ship easily and hid in the cabin, like a monster in the ignoble belly of the colossus. From there, he started ticking in order to terrify his enemy.

> Very frightful was it to see the change that came over [Hook]. It was as if he had been clipped at every joint. He fell in a little

heap. . . . Even the iron claw hung inactive. . . . He crawled on his knees along the deck as far from the sound as he could go. The pirates respectfully cleared a passage for him . . . 'Hide me,' he cried hoarsely. They gathered round him . . . but they had no thought of defending him.'

Hook was faced with his fate. Fate, crocodile, Peter . . .

In the meantime, Peter had released the boys. Only Wendy was still bound to the mast. Peter cut Wendy's bonds and took her place by the mast. This new change of identity enabled him to surprise the pirates. The battle was set: Hook and Peter were face to face.

The others drew back and formed a ring about them . . . For long the two enemies looked at one another; Hook shuddering slightly, and Peter with a strange smile upon his face.

'So, Pan,' said Hook at last, 'this is all your doing.'

'Aye, James Hook,' came the stern answer. 'It is all my doing."

'Proud and insolent youth,' said Hook. 'Prepare to meet thy doom.'

'Dark and sinister man,' Peter answered, 'have at thee.'

Without more words they fell to.

They only stopped when Peter had wounded Hook, piercing him in the ribs.

At the sight of his own blood, whose peculiar colour, you remember, was offensive to him, the sword fell from Hook's hand, and he was at Peter's mercy . . .

'Pan, who and what art thou?' he cried huskily.

'I'm youth, I'm joy,' Peter answered at once. 'I'm a little bird that has broken out of the egg.'

Hook knew that his final moment had come. Seeing Peter slowly advancing upon him through the air with dagger poised, he sprang upon the bulwarks to cast himself into the sea. He did not know that the crocodile was waiting for him . . .

That night, the lost boys slept in the pirates' bunks; all but Peter, who strutted up and down on deck until at last he fell asleep . . . He had one of his dreams that night, and cried in his sleep for a long time, and Wendy held him tight.

THE RETURN HOME

At No 14, the window was open, as it was every night, to welcome the children. The beds were ready and Mr Darling had fallen asleep, as usual, in Nana's kennel. Since the children had left, he had decided that that was his place. That would teach him for being jealous of a dog!

As for Mrs Darling, she had lost her former gaiety. Was it her fault if she was too fond of her children? It was so sad to see her in her chair, where she had fallen asleep, looking so miserable. Her hands moved restlessly on her chest as if she had a pain there.

> Peter reached the window first and he closed it quickly to make Wendy believe that her mother had barred her out. But then he saw the tears in Mrs Darling's eyes.
>
> 'She wants me to unbar the window,' thought Peter, 'but I won't, not I.'
>
> He peeped again, and the tears were still there – or another two had taken their place.
>
> 'She's awfully fond of Wendy,' he said to himself. He was angry with her now for not seeing why she could not have Wendy. The reason was simple: 'I'm fond of her too. We can't both have her, lady.'
>
> But the lady would not make the best of it, and he was unhappy. He ceased to look at her, but even then she would not let go of him. He skipped about and made funny faces, but when he stopped it was just as if she were inside him, knocking.
>
> 'Oh, alright,' he said at last, and gulped. Then he unbarred the window.
>
> 'Come on, Tink,' he cried, with a frightful sneer at the laws of nature, 'we don't want any silly mothers'; and he flew away.

No sooner had they landed in their room than the children slipped into their own beds, although the youngest had some difficulty recognizing his own. Mrs Darling's surprise was even greater to discover them asleep in their beds; she called her husband and Nana to share her bliss.

There could not have been a lovelier sight; but there was none to see it except a strange boy who was staring in at the window. He had ecstasies innumerable that other children can never know; but he was looking through the window at the one joy from which he must be forever barred.

SPRING-CLEANING

When they heard about the lost boys, Mr and Mrs Darling immediately agreed to adopt them. This left Peter. Mrs Darling proposed to adopt him too, but when he learned that the condition of this was to become a man, he refused point-blank. He simply wanted Wendy to return with him to the Never Land. She begged her mother to let her go, as if she felt unable to resist again:

'But he does so need a mother.'

'So do you, my love.'

They finally struck a compromise. Wendy [could] go to him for a week every year to do his spring-cleaning. Wendy would have preferred a more permanent arrangement, and it seemed to her that spring would be long in coming; but this promise sent Peter away quite gay again. He had no sense of time, and was so full of adventures . . .

Wendy must have known this when she said to him: 'You won't forget me, Peter, will you?'

Of course Peter promised; and then he flew away. He took Mrs Darling's kiss with him. The kiss that had been for no one else Peter took quite easily. Funny. But she seemed satisfied . . .

Peter came for her at the end of the first year. She flew away with Peter in the frock she had woven from leaves and berries in the Never Land, and her one fear was that he might notice how short it had become; but he never noticed, he had so much to say about himself. She had looked forward to thrilling talks with him about old times, but new adventures had crowded the old ones from his mind.

'Who's Captain Hook?' he said with interest when she spoke of the arch enemy.

'Don't you remember,' she asked, amazed. 'How you killed him and saved all our lives?'

'I forget them after I kill them,' he replied carelessly.

To avoid suffering, the sad child is forced to 'kill' memories charged with great emotion. The young sportsman unable to enjoy the pleasures of his life spoke about a 'fog' which masked his feelings. Long before, he had experienced emotions that were so unbearable that he had been forced to destroy them. 'See nothing, hear nothing, feel nothing,' he said.

For Peter, Wendy tried not to grow up too fast; she even felt she was untrue to him when she got a prize for general knowledge.

But the years came and went without bringing the careless boy; and when they met again Wendy was a married woman, and Peter was no more to her than a little dust in a box in which she had kept her toys. Wendy was grown up. You need not be sorry for her. She was not of the kind that likes to grow up.'

She had a daughter who was called Jane, and who loved to hear her mother tell her all she could remember about Peter Pan and the fabulous flight:

'The way I flew! Do you know, Jane, I sometimes wonder whether I ever did really fly.'

'Yes, you did.'

'The dear old days when I could fly!'

THE BETRAYAL

One night came the tragedy . . . after the story had been told for the night, and Wendy was sitting on the floor, very close to the fire . . . The window blew open as of old, and Peter dropped on the floor.

He was exactly the same as ever, and Wendy saw at once that he still had all his first teeth. She huddled by the fire not daring to move, helpless and guilty, a big woman.

'Hello, Wendy,' he said, not noticing any difference, for he was thinking chiefly of himself; and in the dim light her white dress might have been the nightgown in which he had seen her first.

'Hello, Peter,' she replied faintly, squeezing herself as small as possible. Something inside her was crying 'Woman, woman, let go of me.'

Peter looked for the two boys in the beds, and Wendy was forced to say:

'That is not Michael.'
Peter looked.
'Hello, is it a new one?'
'Yes.'
'Boy or girl?'
'Girl.'

Wendy realized that he was expecting her to fly away with him. But she knew it was useless to say that she had forgotten how to fly. She rose; and now at last a fear assailed him.

'What is it?' he cried, shrinking.
'I will turn up the light,' she said, 'and then you can see for yourself.'

For almost the only time in his life that I know of, Peter was afraid. 'Don't turn up the light,' he cried.

She let her hands play in the hair of the tragic boy. She was not a little girl heartbroken about him; she was a grown woman smiling at it all, but they were wet smiles.

Then she turned up the light, and Peter saw. He gave a cry of pain; and when the tall beautiful creature stooped to lift him in her arms he drew back sharply.

'What is it?' he cried again.
She had to tell him.
'I am old, Peter. I am ever so much more than twenty. I grew up long ago.'
'You promised not to!'
'I couldn't help it. I am a married woman . . . and the little girl in the bed is my baby.'

'No, she's not.

But he supposed she was; and he took a step towards the sleeping child with his dagger upraised. Of course he did not strike. He sat down on the floor instead and sobbed; and Wendy did not know how to comfort him, though she could have done it so easily once. She was only a woman now, and she ran out of the room to try to think.

'Peter continued to cry, and soon his sobs woke Jane. She sat up in bed . . .'

– and it is easy to picture what happened!

NEVER GROW UP

Poor little sad child! Is he still the hero of the Never Land, or has he become its prisoner? The enigma of the story remains intact: Wendy used the place to help her grow up, while Peter was doomed to repeat adventures and battles forever. Even if the people change, their roles remain identical.

The final image, that of the little boy sobbing at the feet of the grown woman, recalls the picture of the baby Peter Pan tapping on the window-pane. Behind the window is the mother, without whom it is impossible to grow up. Peter faces this inaccessible mother like a child before the coffin of a dead parent.

One grave question remains: how did Wendy succeed in leaving the Never Land while Peter has remained there for ever? We have seen how a disappointment, a moment of sadness, a loss of illusion was enough to make these two children vanish into the Never Land, where everything is possible.

Peter claims that he decided to leave his parents on the day of his birth; he admits that he would have liked to return, but was unwanted. This parental rejection determined the course of his entire existence, and one feels that if he ever became an adult, he would resemble Captain Hook, because he too is familiar with self-hatred.

Does he think that Wendy's presence will change things

in the Never Land? That the love of a little mother will replace the love of his own mother? And that, thanks to this love, he will be able to love himself? Yet Solomon Caw told him that there was no second chance.

For Wendy, the Never Land has another function. Her disappearance serves as a lesson to her parents: for her father, because he lied, and for her mother, her rival, because she did not protect her from paternal deceit. Yet to disappear in this way, the child must have implicit trust in her parents and in their love. Quite often, children who 'cling' most to their mothers are those who are afraid of being abandoned.

When Wendy reaches the Never Land, she already has a well-established sexuality. She has crossed the border between the dream of being a boy and the certainty of being a girl. With her brothers she assumes a femininity, even at the cost of its disparagement, because it is quite natural for each sex to think that it is the best. Furthermore, Wendy, like her brothers, is very surprised when Peter praises the female sex.

Does he want to have her for himself? A sad child needs to believe in the possibility of being both boy and girl, man and woman . . . Wendy is very fond of playing the little mother. This enables her to imitate her mother (for Peter Pan, however, there's never any question of being a father!) and it is certain that this voyage to the Never Land is helping to prepare her for the future.

Yet she does not forget her true parents, and makes an effort to keep their memory alive for her brothers, by telling stories about the family in London.

I believe that these tangible and true elements of her identity enable her to recognize the moment of danger when the Never Land threatens to enclose them; she has the time to decide when to return to reality. She will doubtless always feel a tinge of nostalgia for Peter, but this will not prevent her from growing up and from having a child. The only unknown factor in all this is her husband, about whom nothing is written. In any case, we only have the author's word for this.

4

Forgotten Childhood

When they encounter Peter Pan, most people recognize the little child that they used to be, and that they tend to forget. Childhood memories are like that; one almost wonders whether they ever really existed. We're talking here of very early memories, like that of birth, or of having been held in one's mother's arms, or of having suckled at her breast; or the memory of the time when she went away, leaving us alone, small and defenceless, screaming with despair because we did not know when she would come back.

We all share these experiences, but having grown up we push them into the background and are ashamed to think about them, and we never talk about them. No one is likely to say, for example, even in the most intimate conversation: 'I remember how I slid along the tunnel, and how strange and frightening it was to come out of the warm and sticky egg that was my mother's belly.'

Nobody talks that way! Or they talk about it differently; one dreams that one has passed through a tunnel and that one *must* come out the other side to avoid the risk of being smothered; one wakes up sweating, panting with fear. But it was just a dream.

When a mother brings her baby into the world (an exceptional moment in the life of a woman who, having sheltered another human being for nine months and having shared everything with it, will now let it emerge at the cost of intense, almost volcanic, feelings) she is reminded for a brief instant of her own birth. But the next minute people are taking photographs of the baby, then comes the round of baptisms or circumcisions and, once again, it is as if nothing has happened.

These omissions are strange. Another important subject which no one can talk about easily is the way in which the baby enters its mother belly, and in what form. It is extremely difficult for the child to picture himself, and yet it is crucial for him to know his origins, and if there was any desire in his creation.

Then comes the day of departure, when we must leave our loved ones. This too is unimaginable. The death of a loved one is inconceivable; we are convinced that we shall exist for ever. 'It is very sad that life is like a game of chess,' wrote Freud, 'a false move can force us to give up the game, with the difference that we cannot begin a second time.'

Thus we forget these simple and obvious things; we do not talk about them, but they torment us from the beginning to the end of our days.

ARCHAEOLOGISTS OF THE MIND

Some individuals have spent their lives examining these questions. They have devoted a genuine archaeological effort to them, going back in the prehistory of the mind to retrieve these moments which are lived so intensely, and yet no sooner forgotten. One of these archaeologists was Sigmund Freud, another was the author of *Peter Pan*.

It may seem peculiar to consider these two men together, one a Jew from Galicia who emigrated to Vienna, the other a Scotsman, a Protestant, who emigrated to London. They were born a few years apart, Sigmund Freud on 6 May 1856 in Freiberg, Moravia, and James Barrie four years and three days later, on 9 May 1860 in Kirriemuir, Scotland.

In my opinion what brings these two men together is the fact that both have delved into their personal despair to construct a master work, thanks to their lost childhood. No doubt they had other points in common. Both came from large families. Freud was born in a modest house in Freiberg. He was the eldest son of Amalia, 20 years younger than her husband. His father, a cloth merchant, already had two sons, one married with two children (the second had just been born) and the other one a bachelor, about Amalia's age. His father was not rich, but he had great ambitions for his son. As for Amalia, a fortune-teller predicted that Sigmund would be a great man. Very early in his life he felt he was his mother's favourite, and this impression never left him: 'In my heart of hearts, deep down, the happy child of Freiberg always exists, the first-born of a young mother, nourished with these initial, indelible impressions, shaped by the soil of his birth.'

He also wrote later that the young man that he had been, his mother's unconditional favourite, had drawn from a triumphant self-esteem the seeds of his future success. Sigmund was 18 months old when a second little boy, Julius, was born, who died seven months later. He never regretted the death of his rival: 'The child resents the undesired intruder, the rival. He reproaches him not only for nursing at his mother's breast, but also any demonstration designed to attract maternal care. He feels himself dethroned, spoiled, dispossessed of his rights. He feels a jealous hatred for his little brothers and sisters, and develops rancour against his faithless mother, which he expresses by an unpleasant change in his behaviour. We rarely form a fair perception of the strength of these jealous impulses, of the tenacity with which they persist, and of their influence on our later development.'

A PLACE TO BE TAKEN

At the age of two-and-a-half, Freud suffered a genuine trauma with the birth of his sister Anna. Suddenly his mother disappeared from the house and his half-brother Philip simultaneously dismissed a nurse who took care of him. The little boy desperately searched for the two women who counted most in his life. Philip explained that the nurse had been *eingekästelt*, 'put into a box' (a German expression which means imprisoned, because she was suspected of theft). Little Sigmund begged his brother to release his mother, the prisoner of the large chest sitting in his chamber. When she reappeared, beautiful and slim, with the new rival, Sigmund asked whether it was not his brother Philip who had placed this baby inside his mother. This question, for the little two-and-a-half-year-old boy, became at once important and dangerous.

It is the shadow of these original puzzles, instilled in the mind of the little Sigmund Freud, and forgotten for years, that probably sparked his passionate curiosity and wove the first fabric of psychoanalysis. So many mysteries for a child: his young mother pregnant with a rival; his big brother who seemed strangely implicated; his nephew, older than he, friend and enemy alike; his father who could have been his grandfather.

The disappearance of a mother, the birth of a baby, the death of a father, can disorganize everything for a child and make him lose the sense of security that he first enjoyed. To recover his position, he is therefore tempted to take the place of his parents. Wendy, for instance, dethroned her mother in the Never Land.

Children are not only clever, but they lie in wait for any opportunity to take the place of adults; the least confusion, the smallest chink in the armour, can encourage them to grab power. This gives them the illusion of an advantage over the adult, or at least of occupying a position of strength.

Throughout his life, Freud retained a passionate attachment to his mother. In his theory, he particularly idealized the relationship between mother and son. In his eyes, every intimate and durable relationship is always tinged with ambivalence; in other words, love and hate intermingle at some time or other. The only relationship stripped of these twin feelings is the one between a mother and her son, because a relationship steeped in narcissism is not disturbed by rivalries.

Freud had implicit faith in his relationship with his mother, and he never questioned it, even during his long years of self-analysis. He could never imagine that this love was diminished in any way by the affection his mother felt for her other children. Despite their presence, he knew he was the favourite.

The ambitions that his parents had for him, Judaism, poverty, and this backdrop rich in original fantasies, doubtless contributed significantly to the virtually heroic courage with which he devoted his life to a difficult and original work and study.

THE WONDERFUL BOY

James Matthew Barrie was the ninth child and third son of a family of modest Scottish weavers. Like Freud, he was born in a very small house; everyone lived, slept and ate in two rooms. A poor family, but one in which ambition was not lacking.

The children of David Barrie and Margaret Ogilvy, particularly the boys, were destined for study. David Barrie, a working man, quiet and confident in education, was highly respected in the small closed community of Kirriemuir. Margaret Ogilvy was a strong woman, self-taught in her own way, who had lost her mother when she was eight years old. She then became a 'little mother' for her younger brother David, and housekeeper for her father.

Having arrived late in the brotherhood, James was not particularly celebrated at his birth. The eldest son, Alexander, was already at the university, and his mother was sure of him from the day he was born. But it was the second son, David, on whom Margaret focused all her ambitions and all her secret dreams. He was her favourite. Studious, calm and handsome, there was not a doubt that he was destined for a brilliant career as a Protestant priest, the highest ambition for a mother who had been a member of the 'Auld Licht' (a fundamentalist branch of Scottish Protestantism).

The young David espoused the wishes of his mother; he particularly shone in theology, and it was decided that he would continue his studies in the school where his brother Alexander taught. The pride she felt whenever he achieved good marks helped Margaret to bear his absence.

The winter of 1867 was extremely severe, and the small lake in front of the school in Bothwell froze over. Alexander had given David a pair of skates, which he shared with a friend. On the evening of David's 14th birthday, the children went skating on the lake. When David's friend took his turn he shot off with all the strength of adolescence, and struck David, who fell head first onto the ice and fractured his skull.

There was little hope of saving him, and Alexander sent his parents a telegram to break the bad news. This drama was to mark little James throughout his life. He wrote in *Margaret Ogilvy*, a book devoted to his mother:

> She had a son who was far away at school. I remember very little about him, only that he was a merry-faced boy who ran like a squirrel up a tree and shook the cherries into my lap. When he was thirteen and I was half his age the terrible news came, and I have been told the face of my mother was awful in its calmness as she set off to get between Death and her boy. We trooped with her down the brae to the wooden station, and I think I was envying her the journey in the mysterious wagons; I know we played around her, proud of our right to be there, but I do not recall it, I only speak from hearsay. Her ticket was taken, she

had bidden us goodbye with that fighting face which I cannot see, and then my father came out of the telegraph-office and said huskily, 'He's gone!' Then we turned very quietly and went home again up the brae.'

THE BEGINNING OF THE STORY

One day, his older sister, finding him sitting in front of his mother's closed door, and unable to console him, advised him to tell their mother that she still had another son!

I went in excitedly, but the room was dark, and when I heard the door shut and no sound come from the bed I was afraid, and I stood still. I suppose I was breathing hard, or perhaps I was crying, for after a time I heard a listless voice that had never been listless before say 'Is that you?' I think the tone hurt me, for I made no answer, and then the voice said more anxiously 'Is that you?' again. I thought it was the dead boy she was speaking to and I said in a little lonely voice, 'No, it's no him, it's just me.' Then I heard a cry, and my mother turned in bed, and though it was dark I knew that she was holding out her arms.

James never left his mother from that day on, trying by all possible means to take the place of his dead brother.

A first brother dead; a little sister arrived three years after his birth. When little Julius disappeared, Sigmund Freud triumphed in his place of the favourite son. In the same way, when David disappeared, James took the place of the adored son. Two mothers in deep depression; two veiled maternal glances; two lost mothers, mourning a little child.

At what moment did the story of James Matthew Barrie begin? Was it at his birth, or was it at the age of six when his mother, locked in mourning for her favourite son, assigned him his destiny? In *Margaret Ogilvy* he tells how his life seemed to be plunged in a thick fog for six years:

It was all guess work for six years, and she whom I see in them is the woman who came suddenly into view when they were at an end. Her timid lips I have said, but they were not timid then, and when I knew her the timid lips had come. The soft face – they say the face was not so soft then. In her happiest moments – and never was a happier woman – her mouth did not of a sudden begin to twitch, and tears to lie on the mute blue eyes in which I have read all I know and would ever care to write. Those eyes that I cannot see until I was six years old have guided me through life, and I pray God they may remain my only earthly judge to the last.

What transpired between the lost mother and the son who remained so faithful? Volumes have been written about the life of James Matthew Barrie, the little man who was strangely gay, and yet at the same time so sad. Many authors have been interested in his literary and theatrical career and his tragic personal life.

The days and months spent in his mother's bed listening to her talk about his dead brother brought James Matthew to realize that she derived some comfort from the fact that David, dead so young, would remain a child for ever.

MAGENTA APRON

'The child for ever' thus became the source of inspiration of young James Barrie. When he was not playing the role of his dead brother, he invented a large number of characters whom he enjoyed directing in the laundry behind his house. In reality, he played other roles:

> When I was a very small boy, another as small was woeful because he could not join in our rough play lest he damaged the 'mourning blacks' in which he was attired. So I nobly exchanged clothing with him for an hour, and in mine he disported forgetfully while I sat on a stone in his and lamented with tears, though I knew not for whom.

Throughout his childhood, Barrie thus developed, with insatiable curiosity, an extraordinary capacity and 'a devouring desire to wear the feelings of others as if they were clothes'. He ceaselessly questioned his mother about her childhood:

> Those innumerable talks with her made her youth as vivid to me as my own, and so much more quaint, for, to a child, the oddest of things, and the most richly coloured picture book is that his mother was once a child also.

The childhood of his mother and, so to speak, the child in his mother, were to be Barrie's main inspiration from the beginning of his life to the end. The story of the little orphan in her 'magenta apron' runs through his work in many forms:

> She was eight when her mother's death made her mistress of the house and mother to her little brother, and from that time she scrubbed and mended and baked and sewed . . . all these things she did as a matter of course, leaping joyful from bed in the morning because there was so much to do, doing it thoroughly and sedately and then rushing out in a fit of childishness to play dumps or palaulays with others of her age.

These maternal tales occupied a large part of Jamie's time. They gradually grew in his imagination and prepared the little mother Wendy in *Peter Pan*, the orphan of painted Lady in *Tommy and Grizel*, and many others.

> I soon grow tired of writing tales unless I can see a little girl, of whom my mother has told me, wandering confidently through the pages. Such a grip has her memory of her girlhood had upon me since I was a boy of six.

His father, David Barrie, is strangely absent. Barrie refers to him in passing in *Margaret Ogilvy* as 'a man I'm very proud to call my father'. In *Sentimental Tommy*, the father dies young and Tommy discovers his clothes folded on the chair. He has already forgotten the person who had worn these clothes.

THE BLOOD OF WRITING

With his mother, James also read many adventure books, like *Robinson Crusoe, Tales of the Arabian Nights* and *Treasure Island*. He borrowed them from the library at the price of one penny for three days. Barrie had subscribed to the *Penny Dreadfuls*, illustrated stories filled with tales of adventure, pirates of deserted islands, blood and thunder on every page. One story also mentioned a little girl who sold watercress:

> This romantic little creature took such hold of my imagination that I cannot eat watercress even now without emotion. I lay in bed wondering what she would be up to in the next number. I know not whether it was owing to her loitering on the way one month to an extent flesh and blood could not bear, or because we had exhausted the penny library, but on a day I conceived a glorious idea, or it was put into my head by my mother, then desirous of making progress with her new clouty hearthrug. The notion was nothing short of this, why should I not write the tales myself? I did write them – in the garret – but they by no means helped her to get on with her work, for when I finished a chapter I bounded downstairs to read it to her, and so short were the chapters, so ready was the pen that I was back with the new manuscript before another clout had been added to the rug . . . They were tales of adventure, no characters were allowed within if I knew their like in flesh, the scene lay in unknown parts, desert islands, enchanted gardens, with knights on black chargers and round the first corner a lady selling watercress. From the day on which I first tasted blood in the garret my mind was made up; there could be no hum-dreadful-drum profession for me; literature was my game.

The idea that he would have to grow up one day and abandon the games of childhood were unbearable to little James. For him, the end of childhood meant the end of everything: 'Nothing that happens to us after the age of twelve is worth much.'

Yet the five years he spent at the Dumfries Academy were filled with happiness. It was at Dumfries that he wrote his first play, *Bandelero the Bandit*, which was judged 'immoral' by the pastor, and which gave him some notoriety at the school.

At the age of 17, Barrie stopped growing, just short of 5 feet 4 inches (1.6m). Completely beardless, he still lived like a very young boy. But he was not the only one; his friend, James Macmillan, from whom he was inseparable, was also thin and frail, 'a boy with a frightened look, poorly dressed and fragile'. Like David, he 'remained a boy for ever', and died young.

The two friends took long walks, and talked of poetry, heroism, battles, and the dead things which are said to escape to return to earth during the terrible hour when night meets day:

> One day we wrote something about ourselves in cryptogram and hid it in a crevice in the ruin, agreeing to have another look for it when we were men. So when I was a man I dug for it and found it, having then quite forgotten what it said. But before putting it back I spelt it out. It gave our names and ages, and said that Macmillan and I had begun to write a story of school life, 'by Didymus' . . . School life is not what a boy usually takes as the subject of his first book, and I think there was something rather pathetic in the choice. It was as if we knew already that the next best thing to being boys is to write about them.

THE CONSTRUCTION OF THE NEVER LAND

What is the true story of a life? If we ask an old person to relate his life, he replies, 'Oh, it was so long ago, I've forgotten . . .' He talks about his childhood, naturally. He remembers certain moments and spontaneously offers a bit of history: 'Oh, yes, I remember, when your mother was young and I . . .' Sometimes these images bring tears to the eyes.

Yet he is able to evoke terrible tragedies, like the death of a son, without crying. Emotion seems absent; perhaps it is buried somewhere in a lapse of memory? But these lapses are not empty; the archaeologists of the mind can draw their content into the daylight, if only for a brief moment, just enough to recover the thread of a story.

Like the circulation of blood in the body, psychic continuity ensures the life of the mind. When someone comes to consult an archaeologist of the mind, it is to show him the ruptures, the failings in his life, which made him lose the thread, and to ask to recover its meaning.

Some lives are constructed like a patchwork: two bits are patched together here, there a piece of brightly coloured fabric hides a hole . . . Sigmund Freud was deeply interested in these holes, and in the omissions and oversights concealed within the mind. They enabled him to understand what was wrong with someone. When it becomes possible to reconstruct what has been forgotten, the true thread of the story emerges; the problem lies in finding out where the thread begins.

As we could see when Peter Pan was still a baby in Kensington Gardens, the true thread of a story lies in the strange confusion of feelings that assail us when we begin to live, to feel, and when we cannot express them. At the time, Peter believed that he was still a bird.

For Freud, the beginning of life is marked by 'great sensual pleasure' with the mother. If she is well, if she has accepted her motherhood, she can maintain in her baby the illusion that he can 'have and be everything'. This is her way of compensating for the shock that he has suffered in departing from the comfortable and warm home which was her womb.

To avoid feeling the pain of the passage and the loss of this paradise, the baby becomes very active in the quest for this illusion. But this early pleasure, these feelings of grandeur, are doomed because the expectations which they mask are incompatible with reality. It is impossible to 'have and be everything'. For example, a small boy cannot become the husband of his mother, nor a little girl the wife of her father. Yet this desire emerges at some time or other in every child.

Its unconscious repression can bring about great distress, and immeasurable moral suffering. The feeling of losing love and the ensuing impression of failure deeply wound one's self-esteem and lead to a feeling of inferiority. Often the loss of a loved one later in life reopens this early wound, without any conscious awareness of it.

DANGEROUS GAMBLE

The reality of having to renounce immediate gratification to be able to grow up is the first serious ordeal for the little child. Peter Pan deliberately rejected it, and others do the same without knowing it.

The ability to renounce great pleasure often depends on the time that the child played with his mother. If this time was not long enough or if there was a sudden interruption, the child will be tempted to prolong this period artificially in order to retain the illusion of being 'everything' and will become Peter Pan!

Sometimes, the aim of a whole life, unconsciously, is to recover this lost or never-known paradise. For instance, the man abandoned very early by his parents, who still tries as an adult to retrieve the lost emotions of his childhood. For him, the search becomes so urgent that he leaves his wife and children to live with another couple and their children for many years, with the sole aim of retrieving these moments of early happiness which he succeeds in feeling from time to time.

The Never Land can be thought of as a hole filled with lost objects which the child is incapable of giving up. All these objects have a familiar air, because they also include those of the parents, as if nostalgia were transmitted from mother to daughter, from father to son.

Sometimes, in fact, parents have no more precious 'treasure' to bequeath to their children than the 'evil' which they have themselves suffered, as if they were desperate to share their pain with them. A young woman suffered greatly from the fact that her mother did not love her father, and betrayed him with another man. When the time came for her to find a companion, she picked a man far removed from her own culture and her deepest needs, as if on purpose to despise him and be unfaithful to him. The inevitable happened: their union was filled with violence and suffering, and the children in turn observed the infidelities from which her mother suffered before they were born.

Barrie's mother had lost her own mother at the age of eight. Little Jamie lost his mother in a manner that was undoubtedly much worse than if she had actually died, at the age of six.

When everything becomes disorganized for a sad child, and he loses his childhood, he is forced to find a solution. Faced with such a catastrophic situation, his personal strategy will be to return to the past, to recover the 'all' that made him the master of the world.

I think that after my father died I found the means of preserving this great pleasure; by taking the central place, the one my father occupied with my mother, which is not an easy thing to do for an 11-year-old girl! For some time I deliberately overlooked my own development; I became a very responsible little girl, indeed too responsible.

Since I was very careful to find solutions and to ensure my mother's well-being, I had no time left to do the work necessary to give up my old toys. I clung even more fiercely to the objects of the past, the treasures of my childhood, like my rabbit which had remained imprisoned behind the barbed wire that surrounded Hungary.

MONUMENTS TO DEAD CHILDREN

The Never Land is thus peopled with a multitude of early pleasures, which can no longer be satisfactorily experienced in the present. These objects from the past become museum pieces, beautiful and fragile. Untouchable to others, but equally inaccessible to oneself, all monuments to dead children, jealously preserved by the memory of a great pleasure of the past but never experienced.

If we succeed in finding this sacred tabernacle in the prehistory of an individual and extract from it the objects of the past, so that they can disintegrate or assume another life, one can then begin to understand his real story. Yet the opening of this intimate and secret place is a terribly painful undertaking, and few dare venture therein.

Freud found that writers have a great deal to teach us about these hidden things:

> But creative writers are valuable allies and their evidence is to be prized highly, for they are apt to know a whole host of things between heaven and earth of which our philosophy has not yet let us dream.

In his study of a work of fiction, *Gradiva*, by Jensen, he speaks of a form of forgetting which can be recognized by the force with which the memory can remain buried, despite a very powerful external appeal, as if an interior resistance fought its reappearance.

Yet what remains thus forgotten can some day live again under the influence of an external event, with psychic consequences that result from a modification of the forgotten souvenir, but which remain incomprehensible for the subject.

'You may drive out Nature with a pitchfork, but she will always return,' Freud declared, and the violence of this return depends on the strength with which it has been prevented. *Gradiva* relates the story of a young man who refused to love a woman and fell desperately in love with a Roman statue:

> The author has not failed to show us how the arousing of the repressed erotism came precisely from the field of the instruments that served to bring about the repression. It was right that an antique, the marble sculpture of a woman, should have been what tore our archaeologist away from his retreat from love and warned him to pay off the debt to life with which we are burdened from our birth.

So what is the true story of James Matthew Barrie? The story that others have written about him? The story he wrote about himself? The story of Peter Pan? Freud believes that, in the world of fiction, novelistic or theatrical, we try to retrieve what we have lost in life. In this case, *Peter Pan* holds the central key that might open the Never Land created by James Matthew Barrie.

After all, Barrie himself claimed that he no longer remembered having written the story of Peter Pan. The secret, as we have seen, lies hidden in the holes of forgetfulness.

THE RIGHT KEYS

Peter had lost his mother, but in fact it was he who had left to play with the fairies; when he was ready to return, the window was barred and another child was sleeping in his bed!

James Barrie never left his mother after the death of his brother David. Perhaps, among his forgotten memories, he hid the feeling of having stolen his mother from the dead brother; or, who knows, perhaps sometimes he felt that it was he who had killed his brother, in order to possess finally the mother he so greatly desired.

When someone visits an archaeologist of the mind the keys to the secret doors of his past are sometimes there from the very first meeting. A skilful archaeologist collects them and stores them in a corner of his mind in order to bring them out at the right time, when the person will be capable of using them. It is useless to show them at a time when the person is incapable of recognizing them, thus risking their essential value. Sometimes the archaeologists, especially if newcomers to the profession, are tempted to reveal their talent in exhuming the keys. It is absolutely essential to avoid this power trap.

The first pages of *Margaret Ogilvy* resemble one of these first meetings; the keys to the Never Land are very quickly detected:

> On the day I was born we bought six hair-bottomed chairs, and in our little house it was an event, the first great victory in a woman's long campaign; how they had been laboured for, the pound-note and the thirty-three penny-bits they cost, what anxiety there was about the purchase, the show they made in possession of the west room, my father's unnatural coolness when he brought them in (but his face was white) – I so often heard the tale afterwards, and shared as boy and man in so many similar triumphs, that the coming of the chairs seems to be something I remember, as if I had jumped out of bed on that first day, and run ben to see how they looked.
>
> I am sure my mother's feet were ettling to be ben long before they could be trusted, and that the moment after she was left alone with me she was discovered barefooted in the west room, doctoring a scar (which she had been the first to detect) on one of the chairs, or sitting on them regally, or withdrawing and re-opening the door suddenly to take the six by surprise. An then, I think, a shawl was flung over her (it is strange to me to think it was not I who ran after her with the shawl), and she was escorted sternly back to bed and reminded that she had promised not to budge . . . Thus was one little bit of her revealed to me at once: I wonder if I took note of it.

It seems that little Jamie hardly had the time to be born when his mother's gaze was already turned towards 'the hair-bottomed chairs' which were so important for herself

and the family! *A great victory for this woman*. No sooner
was she left alone with him, than she went off to look at
her chairs – he would have loved to have accompanied her
to cover her with her shawl; it was inconceivable that there
could have been a time when it was not he who covered
her. He could not imagine that he had been a baby. Could
it be that his mother had forgotten to weigh him at his
birth? Yet this scene appeared to him to be so real that he
wondered whether he had not already made notes on the
subject.

The neighbours came to see the little boy and the chairs
(as if both had the same value). Naturally, Margaret agreed
with them, the child would never go to the university; after
all, they were just like them, in the same condition, naturally,
naturally . . . But in these words, spoken over his cradle, did
the baby Jamie already detect the secret wishes of his mother,
the burning ambitions behind the dear face? Because the chairs
were only the beginning:

> And when we were left together, did I laugh at the great things
> that were in her mind, or had she to whisper them to me first,
> and then did I put my arm round her and tell her that I would
> help? Thus it was for such a long time: it is strange to me to feel
> that it was not so from the beginning.

One may remember that Peter Pan had flown off to the fairies
on the day he was born, when he had heard his parents
planning his future.

Jamie seemed to have emerged from his mother's womb
to enter her dreams of grandeur immediately. He was ever
attentive to maternal desire, to the point where he wanted to
go and see the chairs with her, instead of telling her: 'Well,
mother, I've arrived, it is I that you must look at, because, if
you don't, I won't be able to love myself!'

Jamie's life began with Margaret's gaze diverted to inanimate objects, to chairs which decorated the main room of the
house. Poor Jamie! It was the very beginning of the Never

Land – the gaze of the mother, dearly desired but not obtained, an endless search in every woman's gaze – a mother.

THE VICTIM OF TRAGEDY

Wendy knew that not having a mother is a tragedy; Peter simply had no idea what the word meant. This often happens with those who have actually lived through such a situation; they simply do not realize the weight of reality; nevertheless, the emotions, the passions survive the event and make unexpected appearances. For example, one sees them sobbing uncontrollably at the cinema, crying alone among a tearless crowd. Although feelings have been separated from the event, they have remained intact.

For little Jamie, his mother's diverted gaze was a tragedy. We can picture him, like the baby Peter Pan carried naked into the icy Kensington Gardens, deprived of the vital warmth of the maternal fabric. In fact he tried to make up for this by wishing to cover his mother himself, from the very first day.

Had he already renounced becoming a fully-fledged human being, having decided on the day of his birth to sacrifice himself for the fragile, ambitious mother with the diverted gaze? Had he agreed to remain a 'half-and-half', one part for himself, and another for his mother; was he aware of this choice? Or had he forgotten the tragedy, and remained gay, innocent and heartless?

Solomon had predicted that Peter would remain a 'betwixt-and-between'; Jamie gave himself to his mother like the tragic little goat, sacrificed in ancient times during the feasts of Dyonisus; half god, the god Pan, and half devil, the god of lust and putrefaction . . . At the end of *Peter Pan in Kensington Gardens*, a little girl comes to give him a goat to keep him company. A goat for a child, a child as goat, Barrie's childhood sacrificed to Margaret Ogilvy, his mournful mother.

The only evidence of this tragedy are the feelings that are evoked in us as we make our way through the pages of his writing. Like the archaeologist who reconstructs history through the vestiges and objects uncovered by his excavations, the archaeologist of the mind works with words, baring the feelings that they mask, in the search for their hidden meaning:

> Peter called, 'Mother! mother!' but she heard him not; in vain he beat his little limbs against the iron bars. He had to fly back, sobbing, to the gardens, and he never saw his dear again. What a glorious boy he had meant to be to her! Ah, Peter! we who have made the great mistake, how differently we should all act at the second chance. But Solomon was right – there is no second chance, not for most of us. When we reach the window it is Lock-out Time. The iron bars are up for life.

Did James Barrie think he had his second chance on the day when, in his mother's room, as she was mourning the death of her favourite son, he cried: 'No, mother, it's only me', and she stretched out her arms to him with a sob?

Like Peter, who found his place in a thrush's nest, Barrie finally found a niche in his mother's mind, in her Never Land, where the dead children are immortalized. Could he have done otherwise? Was this the only place for him? In any case, once installed, he never left it. Yet he tried to save the half of himself he still possessed: to survive, he started to write.

The wandering child, the lost boys, a little girl who becomes mother, Peter Pan, the little white bird: all James Barrie's characters are the proof of that deep emotion which clung to him like the christening robe, the robe of the lost child searching for his mother from the day he was born and not able to separate from her without losing himself.

THE CHILD DOCTOR

If James Matthew Barrie had a second chance, it was his ability to capture 'the little girl in her magenta apron carrying the bowl to her father' in his writing and never to let it go.

Perhaps in this way he retained the means of becoming 'the wonderful boy he had wanted to be for her', and one of the 'halves' of himself clung passionately to this project. The assurance that she could love the prodigal child gave him hope of ultimately loving himself. Yet he had a second plan, much more altruistic, to cure his mother and to make her laugh:

> After that I sat a great deal in her bed trying to make her forget him, which was my crafty way of playing physician, and if I saw any one out of doors do something that made the others laugh I immediately hastened to that dark room and did it before her. I suppose I was an odd little figure; I have been told that my anxiety to brighten her gave my face a strained look and put a tremor into the joke (I would stand on my head in the bed, my feet against the wall, and then cry excitedly, 'Are you laughing, mother?') – and perhaps what made her laugh was something I was unconscious of, but she did laugh suddenly now and then, whereupon I screamed exultantly to that dear sister, who was ever in waiting, to come and see the sight, but by the time she came the soft face was wet again. Thus I was deprived of some of my glory, and I remember once only making her laugh before witnesses. I kept a record of her laughs on a piece of paper, a stroke for each, and it was my custom to show this proudly to the doctor every morning.

Little Jamie tried so assiduously to comfort his mother, that other members of the family, particularly his sister Jane Ann, Margaret Ogilvy's favourite daughter, actively encouraged him in his task. Jane Ann one day suggested that he speak about the dead child to his mother:

> I did not see how this could make her the merry mother she used to be, but I was told that if I could not do it nobody could, and this made me eager to begin. At first, they say I was often jealous,

> stopping her fond memories with the cry, 'Do you mind nothing
> about me?' but that did not last; its place was taken by an intense
> desire (again, I think, my sister must have breathed it into life)
> to become so like him that even my mother should not see the
> difference, and many and artful were the questions I put to that
> end . . .

Jamie thus set about rummaging in his mother's memory to
learn David's gestures and behaviour down to the tiniest
detail. This game soon became a genuine task for the child,
to which he applied himself with the zeal that a good actor
enlists in preparing his role, as if his life depended on it.

In the same way, Peter Pan in Kensington Gardens 'played
at playing' like a real child; but the real child remained David,
and Jamie was nothing but a false David, an intruder.

One day he felt ready: wearing his brother's clothes, he took
up David's typical stance in front of his mother, legs akimbo,
hands in his pockets, head held high: the posture of Peter Pan!

> I stood still until she saw me, and then – how it must have hurt
> her! 'Listen!' I cried in a glow of triumph, and I stretched my
> legs wide apart and plunged my hands into the pockets of
> my knickerbockers, and began to whistle.

The gesture of this tragic little goat who sacrificed his life to
be able to reach his mother, giving her both pain and pleasure, was the birth of Peter Pan!

Jamie becomes David, Jamie becomes Peter Pan, Peter Pan
is David and Jamie plays at being the dead child.

Peter returned to his sleeping mother's bedside:

> But she looked sad, and he knew why she looked sad. One of
> her arms moved as if it wanted to go round something, and he
> knew what it wanted to go round.

He also knew that he held the secret of his mother's happiness and, without the shadow of a doubt, that he was capable
of giving her the greatest gift that a woman can receive, a
little boy of her own!

All little boys dream one day or another of being able to give their mother a baby, but they give up the idea because they realize that this must be the father's privilege. One wonders if the notion of 'father' even existed for Peter Pan.

THE FINEST GIFT

Jamie gave the gift of the 'wonderful little boy' to his mother: it was himself. But, if the truth were known, he was actually of two minds: 'Sometimes he looked longingly at his mother, and sometimes he looked longingly at the window . . .'

To become her boy again, to become the former Jamie, meant accepting a 'dead' mother, mourning for the other child, and hence becoming a motherless child. To become her 'wonderful boy' again, in other words David, meant undertaking an endless adventure, acquiring the illusion that he could be his mother's favourite and start to exist at the age of six. Yet for this, as for everything else, there was a price to pay: he was going to have wings, but he would never quite be himself again.

Jamie, entering the room, discovered his mother lying in her bed (note the absence of a father barring his way). Peter wanted to please his slumbering mother: 'It would have been pleasant to hear her cries of joy when she would clasp him in her arms, and, above all, how delicious that would be for her!'

However, such a great pleasure offered to a grown woman like his mother can also frighten a little boy. Was it this fear that told Peter not to wake her up? He hesitated to call 'Mother', as he refrained from kissing her, for fear that 'the joy of the kiss' would wake her. He finally found a solution: 'He played her a lovely kiss on his pipe, he never stopped playing until she looked happy and then he flew back to the Gardens' – just as Jamie decided to play for his mother to make her laugh.

It is not possible to hate a sad mother who cries. Yet the child needs to be angry with his mother to prove that she can survive his blows and his hatred. A mother's resistance certifies his own existence, because he too will survive the storm unscathed.

But a sad mother is liable to succumb to such an attack. The sad child is not free to test his mother's strength; he must protect her from everything, even from his own hateful impulses. The fear that she could disappear at any moment keeps him in a fragile state that prevents him from expressing his own desire. Love and hate remain separate and assume a disproportionate scale, because the proof of survival is impossible to obtain. Every feeling becomes dangerous, even murderous.

So the child remains torn 'between two desires'; he wants to have his mother entirely to himself, as in the beginning, and at the same time she frightens him. We saw that Freud believes that every human being is 'between two desires', except the son for his mother. Love between son and mother is untarnished and unambivalent. Did Freud carry this into his theory in order to protect his mother? He too wanted to be the 'wonderful boy', and harboured great nostalgia for the return.

Barrie declared that he could not remember having existed before the age of six. He knew that the 'timid lips' and the 'gentle face' of his mother had not always been thus, as if they could have masked the terrible mother who frightened the little boys at night, as she appeared in their dreams.

How to admit one's fear of a mother whose gaze is veiled by tears? How to hate this deeply wounded woman? For James Barrie and for Freud, only desire was possible towards this particular mother!

THE BRIDAL VEIL

Yet she clearly assumed another form at night. Let us remember: Peter Pan was often very agitated at night, and Wendy had to take him in her arms to calm him down:

When this horrid nightmare got hold of me, and how, I cannot say, but it has made me the most unfortunate of men [writes Barrie]. In my early boyhood it was a sheet that tried to choke me in the night. At school it was my awful bed-fellow with whom I wrestled nightly while all the other boys in the dormitory slept with their consciences at rest. It had assumed shape at that time: leering, but fatally fascinating; it was never the same, yet always recognizable. One of the horrors of my dream was that I knew how it would come each time, and from where. I do not recall it in my childhood, but they tell me that, asleep in my cot, I would fling my arms about wildly as if fighting a ghost. It would thus seem that my nightmare was with me even then, though perhaps only as a shapeless mass that a too lively imagination was soon to resolve into a woman beautiful and cruel, with a bridal veil over her face. When I see her she is still a long way off, but she approaches rapidly. I cower in a corner till she glides into the room and beckons me to follow her . . . Her power is mesmeric, for when she beckons I rise and follow her, shivering, but obedient. We seem to sail as the crow flies to the church which I attended as a child, and there everyone is waiting for us . . .

One hideous night she came for me in a cart. I was seized hold of by invisible hands and flung into it. A horrible fear possessed me that I was being taken away to be hanged, and I struggled to escape . . . My hands were bound together with iron chains, and as soon as I snapped them a little boy with wings forged another pair. Many a time when awake I have seen pictures of that little boy generally with arrows in his hands, one of which he is firing at some man or woman. In pictures he looks like a cherub who has over-eaten himself, but, ah, how terribly disfigured he is in my dreams! He is lean and haggard now, grown out of his clothes, and a very spirit of malignity. She drives the cart, laughing horribly as we draw nearer and nearer the church, while he sits behind me and occasionally jags me with an arrow. When I cry out in pain she turns and smiles upon him, and he laughs in gay response.

Can one possibly measure the colossal energy mobilized by this little boy in order to take the place of the dead child, to make his mother laugh, and to repair the wound at the risk of losing his identity?

The force of the nightmare of the terrible woman, which never left him, shows us the pain of renunciation, at the price of his own sexuality, and the pleasure which he derived by experiencing this suffering with his mother.

We begin to understand how passionately he listened to Margaret's stories. He wanted to take everything from her, and control everything in her (just as Peter Pan became dangerous when he desired Wendy's stories).

EMPTY COSTUME

Margaret Ogilvy's father, 'the only hero of her life', was a stonemason. He was a man worn out by a hard working life, and a serious cough whisked him away nine months before Barrie's birth. Yet all the tales Margaret told Jamie about his grandfather immediately became real for the child, to the point where he describes them in the present:

> It is a night of rain or snow, and my mother, the little girl in a pinafore who is already his housekeeper, has been many times to the door to look for him. At last he draws nigh, coughing . . . Or he is in this chair repeating to her his favourite poem, *The Cameronian's Dream* and at the first lines so solemnly uttered, 'In a dream of the night I was wafted away' she screams with excitement, just as I screamed long afterward when she repeated them in his voice to me.

The sad child who has lost his childhood tries to capture the childhood of a parent, or of other children. I too listened tirelessly to the stories of my mother's childhood: I saw, as if I had been there myself, the huge garden in which she hid to eat apricots, while revelling in the adventures of *The Slave of the Huns* by Géza Gardony . . . The big kitchen table around which the ten children took their meals with their parents . . .

The sunlit morning when grandmother chatted with her daughters for hours around coffee: 'Well, children, what shall we have for lunch today?' And the wonderful stories of Aunt Ethel who was married in Moscow to one of the Tsar's ministers. The gilded satins, the jewels, the bells of the Kremlin, the tinkling of the troïka on the snow . . . 'B-r-r-r-r!' cried Alyosha, bringing the horses to a halt. 'Nianichka daragaja!' exclaimed my cousins when they reached Hungary, fleeing the October Revolution! I didn't need novels; my head was full of my mother's stories!

The death of a parent can plunge someone into the Never Land where everything is possible – for example, where the little girls can become mothers of their brothers and house-keepers for their fathers. Like Peter playing father for the lost boys, one plays at being adult, and one again becomes small; when one becomes big one cannot but remain small . . . because being big remains a game.

One wonders who this grandfather was for little Jamie, the only hero of his mother's life, from whom she had borrowed the cough which would later carry her off too. Was this his spiritual father? Of his true father he said nearly nothing. When he mentioned his parents' marriage, it was as though he spoke of a personal souvenir. Once again, he was outside his child's place (we know that time does not exist in the Never Land!). On the other hand, an accurate description of the father is available in *Sentimental Tommy*; let us judge for ourselves:

> Of this man who was his father he could get no hold. He could feel his presence, but never see him. Yet he had a face. It sometimes pressed Tommy's face against it in order to hurt him, which it could do, being all short needles at the chin . . . There came a time when the man was always in bed, but still Tommy could not see his face. What he did see was the man's clothes lying on the large chair just as he had placed them there when he undressed for the last time. The black coat and worsted waistcoat which he could take off together were on the seat, and

the light trousers hung over the side, the legs on the hearthrug, with the red socks still sticking in them: a man without a body.

Who can rival a man without a body? Jamie's true rival was always David. He knew it when he looked at Margaret sleeping:

> and even while she slept her lips moved and she smiled as if he had come back to her [Peter Pan at the window] and when she woke he might vanish so suddenly that she started up bewildered and looked about her, and then said slowly, 'My David's dead!' or perhaps he remained long enough to whisper why he must leave her now, and then she lay silent with filmy eyes.

It was difficult to hate David, a dead child. It is by writing that James Matthew Barrie avenged himself, bared his teeth and bit whoever he wanted, including his mother. It is thus that he wrote a novella entitled *Dead for Twenty Years* about a similar tragedy in the life of another woman. It was the only story of which his mother never spoke to anyone.

How can one avoid feeling vengeance towards a sad mother? A lost child, now a grown man, related a dream that he had of his mother: 'I see a woman dressed in black. The scene takes place on the seashore, the weather is icy. She wears a veil and dances around me singing: "You have no pupils, you have no pupils!" '

The little 'aviator', who for many years could draw nothing but aeroplanes, had to stop seeing me. He knew from the start that his mother could not tolerate his coming to see me for long. She withdrew him very soon from anything he undertook (even if she had organized it for him). He protected her closely. He always worried about her. One day, we took out the plasticine and I realized that he needed a knife to complete a major task. He started on the plasticine, tearing it, chopping it up and cutting it . . . a real butchery! He then left me, highly content.

THE FIERCE JOY OF LOVING TOO MUCH

There were other children in little Jamie's house, all the babies in whom Margaret placed her hopes: 'I see her bending over the cradle of her first-born, college for him already in her eye.' Then there was a second daughter: was it Tinker Bell, the little fairy Tinker Bell ready to sacrifice her life for Peter Pan? 'What I am sure of is that from the first the child followed her with the most wistful eyes and saw how she needed help and longed to rise and give it.'

Jane Ann so clung to the desire for her mother that she decided to care for her all her life, as if Margaret Ogilvy had assigned her the role of the mother that she had lost at the age of eight. Jane Ann played the role to perfection, and even managed to die before her mother by a few days. Her daily suffering, her pains, were overlooked by all, including herself. When Barrie arrived from London, the two women were already dead.

> I saw her lying dead and her face was beautiful and serene. But it was the other room I entered first, and it was by my sister's side that I fell upon my knees. The rounded completeness of a woman's life that was my mother's had not been for her. She would not have it at the price. 'I'll never leave you, mother' – 'Fine, I know you'll never leave me.' The fierce joy of loving too much, it is a terrible thing. My sister's mouth was firmly closed, as if she had got her way.

'The fierce joy of loving too much' recalls the earliest love when baby and mother are one, before 'the two desires', love and hate, arrive to confuse everything. These are the 'two desires' that complicate life; some people cannot admit that hatred and anger can spoil 'the fierce joy of loving too much'; they think that hatred can be set aside. Like the crocodile prowling around Captain Hook, hatred starts to live a separate life, it is strengthened, it surreptitiously attacks he who pretends to ignore it, it kills those it loves most.

Freud showed considerable interest in the sad child, when the shadow of the loved and lost object falls on him and envelops him. The hatred that the child feels because of this loss is turned against him, attacks him constantly and can even kill him. Self-sacrifice is often the culmination of this interior hatred.

Between a fragile, mourning mother, behind whom a dead mother emerged, a tragic sister, a dead brother and a bodiless father, Jamie could only fear his hatred and the presumed danger which it represented for his loved ones. Later on, many literary critics qualified his writings as 'sadistic'.

SELF-AWARENESS

Rivalry, hatred and inexpressible aggressiveness towards his loved ones do find an outlet in Barrie's writing, as if to help him settle accounts. Peter Pan cuts off Captain Hook's arm; Hook bites Peter; the boys kill the pirates; Peter kills the boys that grow up; and the crocodile is always lurking, with the clock of death ticking away to remind us that every moment counts towards our final destiny.

But it is in *Sentimental Tommy* that Barrie, without any pretence, describes the emotions and the disarray of his life: for instance, the deep despair of a young boy on the birth of an intruder (Maggie, Margaret Ogilvy's second daughter, was born when Jamie was three years old, and she usurped his place as the baby of the family, as Freud had been 'replaced' by his little sister).

Tommy is seated on the stairs with his friend Shovel, in a poor neighbourhood of London where he lives with his mother. The two children see the doctor who comes to visit Tommy's mother: ' "It's a kid or a coffin," he said sharply, knowing that only birth or death brought a doctor here.'

It soon becomes obvious that the imminent arrival of a baby is involved, and Tommy is convinced that he simply has to watch the staircase to prevent the intruder from passing through. We can imagine his disappointment when he finally returns home and his mother, exhausted, deep in her bed, calls him: 'She guessed that he had heard the news and stayed away through jealousy of his sister, and by and by she said, with a faint smile, "I have a present for you, laddie." ' But when she went to show him the baby, he cringes, and cries out: 'No, no keep her covered up!' Like Peter Pan, when Wendy wanted to turn up the light to show him that she had become a woman: 'For almost the only time in his life, that I know of, Peter was afraid. "Don't turn up the light," he cried.' Like the little aviator who came to see me, when we talked about the birth of babies: 'No, no, I don't want to know!'

Tommy, jealous, suddenly deprived of his mother's hands, cries: 'It's true what Shovel says, you don't not love me never again; you jest loves that little limmer!' Like Jamie who accused his mother: 'You only love David!' 'Nah, nah,' the mother answered, passionate at last, 'she can never be to me what you hae been, my laddie, for you came to me when my hame was in hell, and we tholed it thogither, you and me.'

CHOOSING ONE'S HEROINE

The complicity between a mother and her child, especially when it works against the father, is extremely costly. It means the loss of childhood, sometimes the loss of life.

I learned one day about an adolescent boy who heard the cries of his mother in his parents' bedroom. Knowing that she was rejecting her husband's advances, he pushed open the door and struck his father. A few months later, he developed a terrible throat cancer and died shortly afterwards. The parents cursed their destiny, but no one worried about the boy's mental suffering. The boy was the only man who counted in his mother's life.

Day and night, love and hate, to know and not to know; the two desires become one. Jamie wanted to know, and at the same time did not want to know whence babies came ('All babies, before being born, are birds').

We have learned that on the very day of his birth, it comforted him to think that he was already taking care of his mother. Perhaps he would simply have liked to arrive through the window like Peter Pan on that fatal night . . . To admit where babies really come from is to admit also that there is a father and a mother, as well as the desire they feel for each other. Jamie could not, did not want to accept this; his whole life depended on it, because his mother had to be his and his alone.

At the beginning of his writing career, he had read with Margaret that a good novelist must have a perfect knowledge of himself and of a woman close to him:

> My mother said, 'Know yourself, for everybody must know himself' (there never was a woman who knew less about herself than she), and she would add dolefully, 'But I doubt I'm the only woman you know well.' 'Then I must make you my heroine', I said lightly. 'A gey auld-farrant-like heroine!' she said, and we both laughed at the notion – so little did we read the future.

By taking his mother as a heroine, James Barrie said to her, just as his sister had done: 'I shall never leave you.' At the end of *Margaret Ogilvy* he confirms this, and his words bear the weight of the tragedy of a son who has never been able to leave his mother:

> And if I also live to a time when age must dim my mind and the past comes sweeping back like the shades of night over the bare road of the present it will not, I believe, be my youth I shall see but hers, not a boy clinging to his mother's skirt and crying, 'Wait till I'm a man, and you'll lie on feathers', but a little girl in a magenta frock and a white pinafore, who comes toward me through the long parks, singing to herself, and carrying her father's dinner in a flagon.

THE CHILD WHO DOES NOT WANT TO
GROW UP

Barrie did not want, and could not, let go of the image of the little girl who became a mother; all his heroines refer to it – Wendy, Grizel, Mary Rose, Margaret Ogilvy:

> When it was known that I had begun another story my mother might ask what it was to be about this time.'Fine, we can guess who it is about,' my sister would say pointedly.

Margaret would play innocent, and his sister would add that it was high time that he keep her out of the books. Barrie adds that as usual his mother would give herself away, unconsciously:

> 'That is what I tell him,' she says, chuckling, 'and he tries to keep me out, but he canna; it's more than he can do!'

Margaret Ogilvy was perfectly aware of the influence that she and her son exerted on each other. She realized very early that one might not wish to grow up; even she had been unable to live her childhood; her skirts had 'never been short', and her father had remained the only hero of her existence. To grow up, one must be able to let go of one's early images, one's heroes, one's heroines of early childhood, in order to find another hero of a different sex, a different family, with whom, despite everything, one wishes to spend one's life.

Did James Matthew Barrie know that his mother's hold on him would prevent him from loving a woman? There is a very poignant passage in *Tommy and Grizel*, when Grizel, knowing that Tommy has been finally released from the influence of his sister, comes to see him full of love and hope:

> Her arms made a slight gesture towards him, her hands were open, she was giving herself to him. She could not see. For a fraction of time the space between them seemed to be annihilated. His arms were closing round her. 'Grizel!' He tried to be

true to her by deceiving her, it was the only way. 'At last, Grizel,' he cried, 'at last!' and he put joyousness into his voice. 'It has all come right, dear one!' he cried like an ecstatic lover. Never in his life had he tried so hard to deceive at the sacrifice of himself.

But he was fighting something as strong as the instinct of self-preservation, and his usually expressionless face gave the lie to his joyous words. Loud above his voice his ashen face was speaking to her, and she cried in terror, 'What is wrong?' Even then he attempted to deceive her, but suddenly she guessed the truth. 'You don't want to be married!' – 'I want to be married above all else on earth,' he said determinedly, but his face betrayed him still, and she demanded the truth, and he was forced at last to tell it.

A little shiver passed through her, that was all. 'Do you mean that you don't love me?' she said. 'You must tell me what you mean.'

'That is how others would put it, I suppose,' he replied. 'I believe they would be wrong. I think I love you in my own way, but I thought I loved you in their way, and it is the only way that counts in this world of theirs. It does not seem to be my world. I was given wings, I think, but I am never to know that I have left the earth until I come flop upon it, with an arrow through them. I crawl and wriggle here, and yet' – he laughed harshly – 'I believe I am rather a fine fellow when I am flying!'

Barrie is Peter Pan, full of gaiety, flying through the air towards the Never Land. If only he could find a Wendy to accompany him . . . But the image of the wing pierced by an arrow is specifically that of Wendy, wounded by the lost boys while approaching the island.

Even if he wanted to remain a 'little boy for ever', it would be wrong to believe that Barrie was uninterested in girls; to the contrary. Yet he found that they did not pay him enough attention.

School was a place of childhood, and the serious question of 'women' did not really arise. It was at Edinburgh University that he really began to feel the solitude of a man who had remained a 'small boy' among men. This situation offered him the opportunity to watch the others, and to collect these observations as genuine treasures, like a scholar conducting research into beings from another planet. Or Peter Pan, who spied on the real children so that he could learn to play like them. Barrie wrote in his notebook:

> Men can't get together without talking filth.
> He is very young looking – trial of his life that he is always thought a boy.
> Far finer and nobler things in the world than loving a girl & getting her.
> Greatest horror – dream I am married – wake up shrieking.
> Grow up & give up marbles – awful thought.

Poor little half-and-half. One can see from these notes how far away he was from the life of ordinary humans! Just like Peter Pan in Kensington Gardens, he remained between two worlds. To be able to write his books, he tried with all his strength to draw his material from his mother's reminiscences and thoughts. But to live the life of a human being sexuality is a necessity, and perhaps this was lacking in the thoughts of Margaret Ogilvy! In any case, she never talked about it to Jamie, judging such things 'dirty', and wishing to inculcate 'nobler' and 'finer' things in him than the carnal desire of a man for a woman.

BAPTISMAL ROBE

If she didn't think much about men and women, Margaret Ogilvy certainly had babies and mothers in her head. She, who had lost her own mother at the age of eight, nurtured a true passion for little children from very early on, to the point of drawing dress patterns, intended for her future offspring, for hours on end.

Babies and babies' robes were all that was left of her mother, the memory of the warmth of her body, the tenderness of her love. Who knows if Peter Pan was not the baby Margaret Ogilvy, who continued to mourn her departed mother?

Later, on the death of her son David, she reclaimed the robe in which all her children had been baptized and refused to part with it, as if the inanimate object represented more for her than her living child. Like the reminder of an absent love, but which surpasses all love: 'There was nothing in the house that spoke to her with more eloquence than the little white robe,' Barrie remembered. 'After all the children who had worn it, it had remained a baby for ever.' In the hour of her death, Margaret again asked for the robe, and as soon as she had it in her hands, clasped it to herself, on her face, 'the mysterious ardour of motherhood'.

Was it motherhood or rather her own mother which she found with her last breath? Like the babies who cling to a little piece of cloth that emits the odour of their mother, was not Margaret seeking in the baby's robe the trace of her mother departed too soon?

When one has lost one's mother, is it possible to leave her? The essential passage between loving one's mother as a child and loving another human being as an adult is a very difficult one for all children. Is the sad child capable of making the crossing? The 'passers' know how difficult it is for human beings to cross the border of childhood, withdrawing from parental destinies, in order to desire a person of the opposite sex.

Why are we all so much in the grip of parental destinies? Conditioned so much by the words, often unsaid and even unknown, pronounced above our cradles? It is just as if, in leaving our mother's womb, we hurried to cling to these desires, to reassure ourselves that we actually were human beings and not birds.

Those who have not been able to latch on to parental desires, abandoned babies for example, ultimately wonder whether they have not engendered themselves, without parental desire. But this is a terrible thought, because only monsters and some plants can reproduce themselves. Better to hang on to dangerous parental desires than to consider oneself in this way . . .

Yet when parental desires are too deeply buried in the Never Land, they can take an adverse direction, especially if the father or mother were themselves sad children. When parental plans are ignored or denied they can become a matter of life or death for the child. James Barrie must have known this because his Peter Pan flees to Kensington Gardens when he overhears his parents' plans.

But tragically, Barrie failed to derive any benefit from his knowledge, because he succumbed to the wishes of his mother. He remained her little boy forever, never able to experience the supreme adventure of loving a woman.

Is a successful life measured by anything more than the capacity to love? This question lies at the centre of Freud's work; it is also at the heart of Barrie's questions and his writing. The Viennese doctor did not examine his own way of loving; this is perhaps why he could invest so much in research and in analysing this fundamental process in the human being. James Matthew Barrie unfailingly asked himself the question; he was aware of being 'gay, innocent and heartless', and his books all allude to his inability to experience love.

James Barrie took considerable care over his image and, above all, he wanted to be loved. He learned this very early with his mother, and sought admiration ceaselessly. Often, those for whom the image, the reflection of oneself, are the most important, do not have the courage to seek the truth, because the truth is always a little unflattering. Narcissus remains fascinated by the reflection in the water of a young and handsome boy, until age tarnishes his beauty and he dies, without knowing it.

Deep in his heart, James Matthew Barrie had a limitless desire for truth. His indomitable courage touches us more than anything else. The writer knows that his job is to provide a good image of his hero, but Barrie is incapable of this, simply because he has decided to 'lend attention to the things that a real biographer normally relegates to the background'.

5

The Lost Child-Adult: A Wife as Mother

To leave one's mother, one's first love, is no easy matter. Yet for a man it is necessary in order to encounter the other love, the love of a woman. But the sad child, incapable of leaving the mother that he has never had, continues to seek her in all women.

James Matthew Barrie left Kirriemuir behind him, and he left his mother, but never successfully crossed the border. . .

In London, he started a career as a journalist by relating the customs and mores of Kirriemuir, all that he had learned from Margaret. He tried continuously to evoke her laughter and, above all, to fulfil this ambitious little woman's deep desire for a hero of a son.

He surpassed all her expectations, as he succeeded in becoming one of London's most famous playwrights, and was ultimately knighted by the Queen; he became Sir James Matthew Barrie.

Unlike many other men, James Matthew Barrie knew that he was different, that he was a 'betwixt-and-between' but, despite the lucidity of his writings, he was doubtless unaware of the consequences that his 'state' could have not only on himself, but also on many other people:

> He knew he could never be a real human again, but oh! how he longed to play as other children play, and of course there is no

such lovely place to play in as the Gardens . . . The birds brought him news of how boys and girls play, and wistful tears started in Peter's eyes.

One of the first things to do to be 'like others' was to get married. On Monday, 9 July 1894, James Matthew Barrie accordingly took Mary Ansell for his wife. The marriage, simple and discreet, was held in the home of the parents, according to Scottish custom. The couple then left for Switzerland on their honeymoon. Two days later, Barrie noted in his diary:

> Our love has brought me nothing by misery.
> Boy all nerves. 'You are very ignorant.'
> How? Must we instruct you in the mysteries of love-making?

TO DO LIKE OTHERS

Mary Ansell was an actress. Beautiful and seductive, she had been introduced to Barrie as the possible leading role in his second play, *Walker London*. He soon succumbed to her charms, and insisted that she be given the part. Mary appreciated the black humour of the writer, who seldom smiled and ridiculed all he cherished most. She also supported his bizarre moods; he could be extrovert and amusing company, but immediately afterwards he might remain tight-lipped for days on end.

Shortly after their meeting, Barrie started a novel called *The Sentimentalist* in which he observed his relationship with Mary Ansell:

> This sentimentalist wants to make the girl love him, bullies and orders her (this does it) yet doesn't want to marry.
> Her ordering clothes for him, &c. – Motherly feelings.
> His kindliness (weak), he feels for her & keeps the thing going on because doesn't want to make her miserable.

When one gets married for 'make believe', and one pretends

to experience love whereas, in fact, one is 'of two minds', catastrophe ensues. As Freud said, nature soon returns, with its share of 'hatred'; this is Pan's 'devil' side.

When I was 21 years old, it was 'normal' to become engaged, and all my university friends had already thought about getting married. I had neither white wedding dresses nor babies in my head; I had to achieve the destiny that my father had set me, to become a doctor – I wanted to change the world!

This neither prevented me from being interested in men, nor from men from being interested in me! Thus a young and brilliant engineer, the first man in my life, proposed to me. I was of two minds, but he was so insistent (I also think that a part of me wanted to do like the others) that I said yes. We organized a small family ceremony, but from that day on I began to have terrible nightmares; every night I saw murders, blood and giant spiders, and woke up in a sweat.

This went on until the day when I decided to break it off. My friend bought a gun and left for New York, to 'end his days'. Fortunately this dramatization sufficed, and he was able to continue his life. We remained good friends and I recovered my dreams of grandeur. It is strange to see how close death can come when one tries to deny one's feelings.

THE SHADOW OF TRAGEDY

Was it an accident that Barrie's marriage to Mary Ansell took place after a tragic event concerning his younger sister, Maggie? Maggie was engaged to a family friend, the Reverend James Winter. In a gesture of generosity, James Barrie gave the fiancé a horse as a wedding present, but a few days before the ceremony James Winter was thrown by the horse and killed instantly. Maggie reacted as her mother had done in the face of tragedy; she took to her bed and refused to be consoled. Barrie felt terribly guilty, as he had with his mother many years before. He never left the bedside, and shared the tragedy with her. But at the same time, he took notes for a future book – was this a way to protect himself? As if wishing to make amends, he promised his sister he would take care of her for the rest of her life. Fortunately for both, Maggie eventually married her dead fiancé's brother.

James Matthew liked the impression of conformity that marriage offered him; he was content to escape from his solitude, and very proud that men turned around as his pretty wife passed by. He finally felt 'normal', yet he could never be a 'husband'.

As time passed, Mary increasingly played the role of a mother for him, because he wanted to be spoiled and protected. But though she loved the 'little boy' in him, she naturally expected something else: a man, a lover, a husband, a father for the child she desired. Alas, while she could share many adventures with him, she was deprived of this one. She wrote later:

> JM's tragedy was that he knew that as a man he was a failure and that love in its fullest sense could never be felt by him or experienced, and it was this knowledge that led to his sentimental philanderings. One could almost hear him, like Peter Pan, crowing triumphantly, but his heart was sick all the time.

Little by little Mary Barrie gave up the hope that James would grow up to take his place as a man by her side one day. She turned her attention to her dogs, until she met a man capable of responding to her female desire. She wrote:

> When love dies, nothing is more dead, because even those who have known it one day will deny it, or forget that it existed. Yet in this case, love was never truly forgotten. It was wasted, mistreated. It was stifled and neglected, and then legally thrown into the tomb.

James Matthew Barrie took the news of his wife's liaison with another man as a terrible catastrophe. He would never have believed that such an event were possible, and he begged Mary to deny the rumour. When she retorted that it was true and that she wanted a divorce, he was totally downcast. Without Peter Pan realizing it, Wendy had tired of his incorrigible indifference.

A sad child is unaware of the harm that he can do to someone he loves; he cannot feel the tragedy. For him, all is adventure: Peter, for instance, could fly thanks to the fairy Tinker Bell who guided him everywhere; she was part of his environment. He could therefore hurt her and be unfaithful to her, without ever doubting her feelings for him! Similarly, during the flight to the Never Land, he sometimes forgot Wendy's existence completely, and went off on an adventure, and failed to recognize her on his return.

Some women tell me that their husbands act as if they could not see them; they have melted into the landscape. Others complain that their companion has developed a habit of doing whatever he wants, but cannot bear the thought that in turn they wish to take a holiday alone with a female friend.

There are also many Wendies who like to play 'little mother' for their boy husbands. Provided that he is happy, even if it is with other women, they are always happy for him! Thus Mary played the role of Wendy for James Barrie for many years: he, in fact, though he did not fulfil his role as a husband and remained impassive to the amorous needs of his wife, was certainly interested in beautiful women, especially when they were accompanied by children.

A MODEL FAMILY

The fatal meeting with the Llewelyn Davies family seems accidental but, on closer consideration, it was inevitable! James Matthew and Mary were walking with Porthos, their Labrador, in Kensington Gardens. The little man, wearing a huge black cloak, with his pretty wife by his side and the big joyful dog, could not fail to attract the attention of passers-by.

Thus two little boys wearing red berets started a conversation with them.

Shortly afterwards Barrie noticed a very beautiful woman, Sylvia Llewelyn Davies, at a soirée at the home of a fashionable lawyer, Sir George Harris. Being in a sociable mood for once, he had accepted the invitation. There was no cause for regret on his part, because he found himself seated at a table beside this beautiful woman.

Apart from the photographs and paintings which depict her, Sylvia has been described thus by a contemporary:

> Without being strictly pretty, she has got one of the most delightful, brilliantly sparkling faces I have ever seen. Her nose turns round the corner – also turns right up. Her mouth is quite crooked . . . Her eyes are very pretty – hazel and very mischievous. She has pretty black fluffy hair: but her expression is what gives her that wonderful charm, and her low voice.

During dinner, Barrie was intrigued to see Sylvia putting sweets into her bag, and asked her for whom they were intended. 'It's for Peter,' she replied, as if this were the most natural thing in the world. Thus began a conversation which revealed that Sylvia was talking with the man with the persistent cough who amused her children in Kensington Gardens. She was the mother of the boys with the red berets.

'There never was a simpler happier family [than the Darlings] until the coming of Peter Pan,' wrote James Barrie in *Peter and Wendy*. Was he describing his arrival in the Llewelyn Davies family?

Arthur Llewelyn Davies, Sylvia's husband, was a young lawyer, brilliant and ambitious, offspring of a 'good Protestant family'. Sylvia's parents were George and Emma Du Maurier, a rather Bohemian and artistic couple (George Du Maurier was a caricaturist for *Punch*), who saw the funny side of life. Sylvia's mother found Arthur a bit too serious for her daughter, who was so gay and so extrovert. But he was very handsome.

The Llewelyn Davies family offered James Barrie an ideal opportunity to pursue all his fantasies. After the failure of his life as part of a 'normal couple', he could both continue to play with children and seduce a mother.

Ah! If only we could remain gay, innocent and heartless for ever! James Matthew Barrie may have turned to the Llewelyn Davies family, his Darling family, in the hope of achieving this fantasy.

When he met them, Arthur and Sylvia already had three boys: George, aged five; Jack, aged four; and Peter, still a baby. Yet George, the eldest, was not his first 'victim'. Barrie had already met other children at his friends' homes such as Margaret, the daughter of the writer W E Henley. She called Barrie 'my friendy', but she pronounced it 'my wendy', which gave rise to the unprecedented Christian name of 'Wendy'.

There were also his two nephews, Charlie and Willie. Charlie was very handsome and intelligent, which greatly pleased the writer, as did his anarchistic and deliberately destructive temperament. For Barrie, the character of the children was 'inspired as much by the devil as by God'. He enjoyed their contradictions, their unlimited appetites, their lack of morality, their self-sufficiency, their ingratitude and their cruelty, alongside the gaiety, the warmth, the tenderness and the sudden waves of emotion, instantly forgotten. And he knew very well how to win their affection by behaving in the same way himself.

IRRESISTIBLE INTRUSION

Yet Arthur Llewelyn Davies was reluctant to accept James Matthew Barrie's passion for his sons. He would have liked to have moments alone with his family when he came home from work in the evening, and he was not always happy to see the little man in his home. To tell the truth, he didn't know how to get rid of him! He also had to resist Barrie's persistent generosity, because the writer was ready to give the children and their parents everything that they could possibly desire!

Barrie did not conceal his great admiration for Sylvia, whom he described in his diary as a 'glorious woman . . . whom one can trust. No question of sex', he added in parentheses.

No sex! What a comfort for Jamie to know that this woman did not expect that of him. She was close, beautiful, a mother of five boys, she had a husband whom she loved and who adored her. Jamie enjoyed every moment spent in her company; he took many photographs of her and her sons, and the boys gradually became the heroes of his writing. He wrote about their gestures in his notebooks, each smile, each tear, to bring them later into their true light, the creation of his painful fantasy. Concerning George, for example, the model of the *Little White Bird*, he wrote: 'I could forgive him everything, except his youth.'

Why did the Darling/Davies family open the window and let this strange little man into their home? Was Sylvia, like Wendy, seduced by the great need for motherly love that she must have unconsciously felt in James Barrie? Did she give in to the worldly pleasure of playing with the famous playwright and enjoying the flattery of his compliments? She certainly knew nothing of the diabolical conflicts which were taking place in his tormented mind. Mrs Darling had felt the danger that Peter Pan represented; Sylvia was unaware of it.

Jamie remained on the window-sill at first, where he could observe at leisure, taste, take and dominate the family. But he remained excluded from the lost love of his childhood. He continued to play, as he had always done: at being everything for his mother, for a mother. For Sylvia's fifth wedding anniversary, he pretended in a letter that it was the day of his own wedding. He succeeded in going back in time as he had already done with Margaret Ogilvy – he could not be excluded from such an event!

Dear Miss Du Maurier,

And so you are to be married tomorrow! And I shall not be present.
You know why.
   Please allow me to wish you great happiness in your married
life. And at the same times I hope you will kindly accept the little
wedding gift I am sending you . . . It reaches you somewhat late,
but that is owing to circumstances too painful to go into.
   With warmest wishes to you and Mr Davis,
   Believe me, dear Miss Du Maurier,
   Yours sincerely,

J M Barrie

THE PRINCE OF THE FAIRIES

Barrie shared his literary successes with 'his family', and
especially with Sylvia, whom he once took to Paris for the
opening night of one of his plays. It was a solitary Arthur,
probably a bit unhappy, who wrote to his father:

> I don't know what your arrangements are for Christmas, nor if
> you are likely to have the vicarage very full. I should like to
> come, if possible, bringing one boy or perhaps two . . . Sylvia is
> at present on a trip to Paris with her friends the Barries, by way
> of celebration of the huge success of Barrie's new play and new
> book . . . they seem to be living in great splendour and enjoying
> themselves very much

'If only we had not accepted this dinner invitation!' lamented
Mr Darling when he discovered, that his children had left for
the Never Land with Peter Pan. Was this also Arthur's great
regret?
   In May 1906, nine years and some months after the famous
dinner where they met Barrie, Arthur Llewelyn Davies fell
gravely ill; a rare tumour was discovered in his mouth, and
an operation deprived him of speech. This tragedy served

James Matthew Barrie well, because it enabled him to take root even more firmly in the Davies family.

He visited Arthur, read him the newspapers, and offered him all the services that he needed. Sylvia wrote to her son Michael for his sixth birthday: 'Mr Barrie is our fairy prince, much the best fairy prince that was ever born, because he is real.'

Jamie was again beside a woman faced with the death of a loved one. Was this a repetition of the tragic moments of his childhood? By becoming so deeply involved in the life of the Llewelyn Davies family, was he trying to thwart destiny?

It is always strange when tragedies are repeated, and we find ourselves in the mysterious *déjà vu* which makes us lose our bearings. I experienced this when I returned to Hungary for the first time with my mother, and we were welcomed by barbed wire fences and soldiers, with machine guns on their hips. We had Canadian passports. Suddenly, although we had waited for hours to be 'inspected', I was seized by two equally violent and contradictory desires: to turn around, go back and never return; or to jump over the barbed wire screaming, hands stretched to the sky: 'Come on, kill me, let's put an end to this barbarity!' I think that this fantasy satisfied me, because I continued to wait until our turn came.

It is difficult to know what James Matthew Barrie felt during this tragedy: was he divided between the desire to love, to cry, to have pity . . . and the desire to kill, to possess, to take the place finally of the father – finally to have his own boys? In the Never Land, the only rule is 'kill or be killed', 'eat or be eaten'.

Subsequently, the Davies' sons tried to understand the circumstances which had surrounded the death of their father. Peter Davies, as an adult, wrote about his family gathering information from various sources of correspondence. His proposed book was curiously called *Morgue*, but he never published it. He commented thus on his parents' relationship with the writer: When the situation became very serious:

JMB stepped in to play the leading part; and played it in the grand manner . . . I can sympathize in a way with the point of view that it was the last straw for Arthur that he should have had to accept charity from the strange little genius who had become such an increasing irritation to him in recent years. But on the whole I disagree. We don't really know how deep the irritation went; and even if it went deep, I am convinced that the kindness and devotion of which JMB gave such overwhelming proof from now on, far more than outweighed all that, and that the money and promise of future financial responsibility he was so ready with – and with what charm and tact he must have overcome any resistance! – were an incalculable comfort to the doomed Arthur as well as to Sylvia in her anguish.

THE OUTSTRETCHED HAND

But Jack, the younger brother, felt differently:

I couldn't at all agree that Father did anything but most cordially dislike the Bart. I felt again and again that his letters simply blazoned the fact that he was doing all he could, poor man, to put up a smoke screen and leave Mother a little less sad and try to show her he didn't grudge the Bart being hale and hearty and rich enough to take over the business . . . I've no doubt at all he was thankful, but he was a proud man, and it must have been extraordinarily bitter for him. And altogether too soft and saintlike to like the little man as well.

Arthur Davies could not speak, and he communicated in writing with James Barrie, who hardly ever left his bedside:

What have the boys been doing? I leave it entirely to you subject to Sylvia's wishes. No one has done so much for me as you have. Give me your hand . . .

All along, the writer, at the sick man's bedside, continued to take notes, identifying with Arthur:

Dying man's fears to friend that he may break down & blubber at end – weakness may master him . . . His idea wd have liked to have children . . . to live on in them. Speaks to friend (a father) about great difference in dying if you have children (yourself living on) – if you haven't you go out completely.

Once again he is installed in the place of the other person, the other now approaching death. He hurries to take away his children, because it is *he* who 'would have loved to have children – continue to live in them'. Captain Hook stretches his claws . . . ready to seize the other's treasure.

Peter Davies relates in his private notes the time when the children learned about the death of their father from their grandmother:

I believe the meaning of her words penetrated pretty clearly to one's immature brain, though not of course their full and permanent significance. It was, as I remember it, a dull and windy day, and I recollect wandering up to the night nursery and staring out of the window for long minutes in vague wretchedness and gloom, at the grey sea and the distant *Gull* lightship . . . 'A boy's will is the wind's will' and as likely as not I was digging on the sands as usual the next morning. But for the moment I think it was borne in on me that a disastrous thing had overcome us.'

ACT AS IF . . .

Despite the shadow of the undeniable tragedy, life continued after the father's death. Things even seemed to go along 'as if nothing had happened'. The children played and attended school; James Matthew Barrie was always present and contributed considerable financial help. Sylvia tried not to make too much of a show of suffering.

The little boys are loving and thoughtful and I always sleep with George now – & it comforts, more than I can say, to touch him, & I feel Arthur must know. He will live again in them I feel & that must be my dear comfort till I go to him at last.

Two days after the Barries' divorced, Peter Davies saw his mother faint and fall in the stairway of the house in Campden Hill Square. The diagnosis was irrevocable: cancer, too near the heart to operate. Yet the pretence must continue; Sylvia must not know the gravity of her state. Her illness was less impressive than her husband's because she did not undergo an operation, but her health declined very rapidly. Soon she had to be carried in a chair. At Christmas, when the children came home for their holidays, they found their mother confined to her bedroom. Despite the 'as if nothing had happened,' they knew that tragedy was striking again.

James Barrie was constantly at Sylvia's side, resuming the role that he had played beside Arthur, three years before. At the same time, he revised his manuscript of *Peter and Wendy* and took copious notes:

> The dying. Friends around talk of other things. Wonder about dying, when silent really makes preparations for dying – for the journey.
>
> One thinks of the dead as a bird taking lonely flight. I saw we would realize it is always one of a great flock of birds.
>
> Man who brings up 4 girls as guardian (better than boys?)
>
> The second chance: beware or you may get what you want.

What wishes? The wish to be at the bedside of a dead mother for the second time, to experience the sadness of the little boy who has lost his mother? So many sad children, so many lost childhoods. Or was it the wish to be finally alone with the boys, playing at being father and mother all at the same time?

A DEAD MOTHER

Sylvia Llewelyn Davies died on 27 August 1910, with her mother, Emma Du Maurier, the doctor, the nurse and Barrie at her death-bed. The boys had gone fishing in the river.

Peter Davies remembers (in his memoirs) his return to the house in the late afternoon, and the shock that he felt on discovering drawn curtains at all the windows. James Barrie awaited him in the entrance, totally heartbroken, and gave him the news with desperate words:

> Poor Jimmy; I think it was I that propelled him, as much as he me, into the room on the left of the little entrance hall, where we sat and blubbered together. Good cause for blubbering too, for both of us; but I remember, and wish I didn't, sobbing out 'Mother! Mother!' at intervals during the sad and painful scene, and realizing, even as I did so, that this wasn't altogether natural in me – that, though half involuntary, it was also a half-deliberate playing-up to the situation.

Nico, aged seven at the time, approached Sylvia's bedroom with the intention of entering, as usual, at tea-time, but he was rudely expelled by one of his brothers, Michael, and fled crying hysterically: 'Cruel God! Cruel God.' At the time, George had not yet returned from fishing. As for Jack, he also became angry, but with James Barrie:

> I was taken into a room where [Barrie] was alone and he told me she was dead. He also told me, which angered me even then, that Mother had promised to marry him and wore his ring. Even then I thought if it was true it must be because she knew she was dying. I was then taken in to see her and left with her for a bit. She looked quite natural, as she'd always been so pale, very lovely and asleep.

Had Barrie told the truth, or was it a product of his hyperactive imagination? Did Sylvia seriously consider marriage with the small, strange, faithful creature? We shall never know. But Peter, in his memoirs, felt that a union between Sylvia, still so beautiful at forty-four, widow of the splendid Arthur, and the little man who adored her and who surely dreamed of stepping into Arthur's shoes, would have been 'a true affront to common sense, for any reasonable person'.

Peter had no memory of the funeral but, on the other hand,

he remembered that the writer had given them new fishing rods on the same morning:

> And I dare say it worked well enough, and that the new rods helped, as no doubt JMB with generous cunning knew that they would, to do the trick. At any rate one seems to remember quite enjoying oneself, flogging the little upland streams and hauling out the little trout, and putting the lowly worm behind one for ever.

'Mrs Darling was dead and forgotten,' wrote James Matthew Barrie at the time in *Peter and Wendy*, while simultaneously watching the boys fish in the rivers!

6

Captain of the Lost Boys

Peter Pan or Captain Hook? Barrie was finally alone with the lost boys; he was sole master of their fate. I believe that we have serious cause for anxiety about the future of the Davies' sons, caught between a fantastic, cocky and oblivious Peter Pan, and a cruel Captain Hook, depressed and unsure of himself.

Immediately after Sylvia's death, James Barrie let the Du Maurier family know of his intention of becoming the children's 'tutor'. To ensure that this would happen he had falsified Sylvia's last will by replacing the name 'Jenny', the sister of the governess Mary Hodgson (whom Sylvia wanted to live in her house) by 'Jimmy'! He thereby gave himself the right to consider 23 Campden Hill Square as 'his' home.

Mary Hodgson protested strongly: like Nana with Peter Pan, she believed that the writer was dangerous for the boys; nor had Emma Du Maurier ever liked him, and all his generosity and gentleness had not changed her opinion. But, despite this opposition, the family remained powerless in the face of Barrie's determination.

Once assured of his role as tutor, he set to as best he could. Nothing was too fine for 'his boys': the best holidays, the best leisure activities, the best clothes and, above all, the best schools – Eton and Oxford, where the élite of English society were trained. James Barrie had never been ashamed of his modest origins (from which he drew inspiration in his writings), but he secretly admired the aristocracy with which he flirted thanks to his literary success. The fact that he was sending 'his boys' to the leading public schools of England gave him tremendous satisfaction.

Yet, despite this tender concern, James Matthew Barrie irresistibly drew the boys to the Never Land, not to enable them to grow up, but to take from them what he himself had lost. In *The Little White Bird*, George, the eldest of the Davies boys, supplied the model of David, the hero. The book is written in the first person by Captain W, 'an old bachelor, pleasant, whimsical and solitary', who is also a writer and who takes regular walks in Kensington Gardens with his dog Porthos. His secret ambition is to have a son whom he could call Timothy. Since he is incapable of realizing this wish himself (he cannot cope with intercourse with a woman), he insinuates himself into the life of a poor young couple by helping them financially, but in an occult fashion.

When the couple expect a child, the Captain observes the matter closely and, when the father announces that it is a boy, the Captain, to be like him (to be normal) tells him that he also has a son, whose name is Timothy.

TIMOTHY AND THE FIVE BROTHERS

When Sylvia died, George was 17 years old, and he thought of Barrie as a close friend. Jack was the only one who opposed Barrie's adoption of the boys. Was it because, unlike the other Davies boys, he had never inspired the writer? However, he accepted the solution of tutorship by Barrie. Peter was 13, and bore the fatal Christian name of Peter Pan. Shortly after their mother's death, he entered Eton, where he was soon subjected to merciless teasing by his classmates, convinced that he was 'the real Peter Pan', until he derived a genuine phobia for the play, calling it a 'terrible masterpiece'.

But it was with Michael that Barrie entertained the most complicated relationship. Michael was born shortly after the playwright's arrival in the Davies family. One could presume that the strange little man seized this opportunity to behave as though Michael were his son. After all, *The Little White Bird* furnished a scenario which he could enter. This is the opinion of Denis Mackail, a contemporary of Barrie, struck like others by 'Barrie's mesmerizing power, always irresistible when he has made his choice'. According to him, the little boy, lively, intelligent and handsome, represented everything that the magician admired most, and he was undoubtedly his favourite.

As to Nico, the youngest, he was seven when his mother died, and was apparently the least affected by the disappearance of his parents. He was also charming, extrovert and affectionate. Like Michael, he considered Barrie neither as a father nor as a brother, but simply as 'just the person I always hoped most would be coming in to see me'.

In the meantime, the writer was preparing *Peter and Wendy*:

> Then [the lost boys] went on their knees, and holding out their arms cried, 'O Wendy lady, be our mother.'
>
> 'Ought I?' Wendy said, all shining. 'Of course it's frightfully fascinating, but you see . . . I have no real experience.'
>
> 'That doesn't matter,' said Peter, 'What we need is just a nice motherly person.'
>
> 'Oh dear!' Wendy said, 'You see I feel that is exactly what I am. Very well, I will do my best.'

LOVE AND HATE

All the time playing at 'mothers and fathers', which must have satisfied the demonic side of the god Pan, in other words by being what Freud calls the 'archaic father of a primitive horde', James Matthew Barrie pursued his self-observation, his search for truth. His dreams continued to torment him and he scrupulously noted them down in his diary; for example, he woke suddenly, petrified with fear, sure of having felt the sheets move:

> I move body slightly – movement of thing stops. Long pause; then it resumes, gentlest possible pushing of me – I resist without pushing back. Pause. Pushing resumed. Electric lamp near me, I set teeth for courage to turn on light – queer idea I won't be able to do it – I push out hand to – hand is stopped by something limp which doesn't push but just prevents – later it makes my hand always miss lamp – I feel being pushed now – no sound of breathing. Then feel stronger attempt evidently to push me out of bed. At last I rushed from darkness to mother's room [she has been dead many years] & cried to her about my degenerate self – thing I have evolved into trying to push me out of bed & take my place. Till that moment of telling I had no idea what the thing was.

Could this 'degenerate self' of James Matthew Barrie have been the sad little child who continued to weep in the ageing body? It is strange to find that Freud tells the same story: love and hate are found side by side. The life wish is accompanied by the death wish; construction is accompanied by destruction.

When aggressiveness is blocked by external obstacles or for interior reasons, this situation can be experienced as a grave injury, and the force of repression is likely to recoil against the subject himself and destroy him . . . A bit like the crocodile ceaselessly pursuing Hook to devour him . . .

ILLNESS À LA CARTE

A little old sad child came to tell me her story. She was so small, with such a gentle voice, that I felt instinctively that, deep down, she had to be a great destroyer. She told me how she had been abandoned by her parents at the age of four, when she had been hospitalized for a grave illness. She had been given up for lost, and her parents, who lived abroad, did not come to see her. But she did not die. Her convalescence lasted many years: she had practically forgotten her family, and spent her time making up stories. One of her favourite games was the story of a girl who was beaten by her mother.

Once cured, she returned to her family, pursued brilliant studies and, later on, married the man of her choice, against her parents' wishes. The marriage was rather a success for her, because she found in her husband a considerable degree of violence which she herself also had, but had never been able to express. She had many children but, by ill luck, each of them nearly died as a baby, either by poisoning or from starvation. Every time, she saved them at the very last minute, when she managed to summon up everything that remained in her desire to see them survive.

When they became adults, they continued nevertheless to 'please' their mother by being often gravely ill, and smoking and drinking. Fortunately, the father had transmitted to them his robust constitution and his violent opposition to their mother, thus enabling them to resist!

Freud was deeply interested in people in whom the same actions were perpetually repeated, at their own cost and at the cost of others, as if they were pursued by an inexorable fate. He called this a 'demoniacal compulsion to repeat' because, in closely examining the situation, it seemed obvious that this 'fate' had left nothing to chance.

A mother came to see me shortly after the death of her son at the age of 23. She was unable to mourn for him and spoke to me about a black fate which bedevilled her family. At the age of 10 she lived in England. Vaccinations were not compulsory for the children, and her mother decided not to have them vaccinated. During an epidemic of diphtheria, this woman and her four brothers and sisters fell ill. Her favourite brother, five years younger than herself, died.

Later on she had five children, like her mother, of whom the eldest boy closely resembled the dead brother. Naturally, he had also been given the same name. She got on badly with her husband and did not spare her children all the complaints she had against him; he reminded her of her bad relationship with her own father, who spent his time gardening to avoid family quarrels. Little by little, the eldest son took the place of the man alongside this woman. He died stifled, like the brother, not by diphtheria, but by a tumour of the throat!

Is it possible to mourn a dead child? Is it possible to mourn a dead mother? These losses criss-cross the Never Land. Sylvia 'Darling' was dead and forgotten, but everyone acted as if nothing had happened, as if life could simply continue.

THE DOUBLE

Towards the end of April 1913, Michael also entered Eton. Whereas George had adjusted to his new environment within a few days, Michael was very unhappy, and was terribly homesick. He missed Mary Hodgson. He missed Uncle Jim. But, more than anything, he missed his mother. For three years, Barrie had done his best to take her place; not a single day passed but he accompanied the child to school, played with him at billiards or cricket, or helped him through his nightmares.

But now that Michael was alone, without Barrie to fill his head with other thoughts, he languished for the contact of the 'vanished hands'. He tried desperately to disguise his feelings, hiding behind a shield of reserve, or trying to mask his depression with bleak humour, like that of his tutor. Barrie wrote later: 'I think few have suffered from the loss of a mother as he has done.' In the hope of filling this solitude, he proposed to write every day, instead of once a week, as he did with George. By the time Michael left Eton 2,000 letters had been exchanged.

The sad child cannot abandon the dead parent. Even if he forgets, if he tries to act as if nothing has happened, he constructs a living tomb within himself; little by little, the tomb and he become one. The sad child behaves like the cannibal: he eats the dead person, and then he feels guilty for having killed him. He must therefore punish himself for his crime, he is tormented, he suffers, but, at the same time, he is avenging himself on the dead person, making the dead person suffer and thus, in a perfectly contradictory way, he derives satisfaction from this suffering.

This is another facet of Hook's vengeance. James Matthew Barrie found his double in this game with himself, and the double was Michael. We have seen how the relationship was based on the confusion between Barrie's imaginary child and the real child. To express these secret feelings, the writer dedicated a book to Michael: *Neil and Tintinnabulum*, the story of a gay, innocent and heartless little boy, Neil, who, having reached adolescence, loses confidence in himself and becomes a different person, Tintinnabulum.

Michael also fuelled the fantasies of James Matthew Barrie in another way in his quest for a double: like Barrie, he was prey to terrible nightmares. This mirror of his own nocturnal life gave Barrie the inspiration for Peter Pan: 'Sometime he [Peter Pan] had dreams, and they were more painful than the dreams of the other boys. For hours, he could not get rid of them and he wept pitifully. They concerned, I believe, the secret of his existence.'

PROHIBITED TO GROW UP

James Matthew Barrie would have liked to play his role as the 'mother' of the boys forever; yet inevitably they grew up. George was already 20 and was infatuated with a young girl of good family, Josephine Mitchell-Innes, whom he wanted to marry. Barrie didn't know what to do: in the Never Land, it is prohibited to grow up . . .

This ideology also had real consequences for the play *Peter Pan*, performed successfully in London ever since its creation. Pauline Chase, the actress who played the role of Peter Pan, reported to the journal *Peter Pan's Post*:

> Every December a terrifying ceremony takes place before Peter Pan is produced, and this is the measuring of the children who play in it. They are measured to see whether they have grown too tall, and they can all squeeze down into about two inches less than they really are, but this does not deceive the management . . .

This reminds us of Peter Pan's words about the lost boys: 'When they grow I kill them.'

On 4 August 1914, Great Britain declared war on Germany. George, Michael and Nico were on holiday with Barrie in Scotland, far from the news with which all Europe was burning. George, already enlisted, persuaded his brother Peter to join up with him. While awaiting their call-up, they continued to live as before. The boys fished and took long walks.

On the first day of training, while they were getting ready, George said to his brother: 'Well, young Peter, for the first time in our lives, we're up against something really serious, **** me if we aren't.' Was it the sad child in him who sensed the coming tragedy? Had he picked this destiny for interior reasons? Or was it pure chance?

James Matthew Barrie opened his wings wide to try to protect his lost boys. He was particularly present, generous and anxious since the danger, on this occasion, came from the exterior.

The letters exchanged between George and Barrie at the time provide an indication of the depth of the relationship between the two men: 'My dear George,' wrote Barrie, 'your letter comes and I know, you are off. It is still a shock to me. I shall have many anxious days and nights too, but I only fall into line with so many mothers.'

The last letter that George received while he was alive was dated 11 March. Barrie advised him of the death, at the front, of Guy Du Maurier, Sylvia's brother: 'Of course I don't need this to bring home to me the danger you are always in more or less . . .'

George was killed on 15 March 1915, in a column marching to Saint Eloi. He must have had a premonition of death, because he had just told a comrade next to him that he wanted to be buried where he fell. That evening, he was seated with the others in the trenches when a bullet went through his head, killing him instantly.

A few days after his death, his answer to his tutor's letter arrived; the tone was reassuring, flippant: 'And if I am going to stop a bullet, why should it be with a vital place?' So Peter Pan, standing in grave danger on his rock, exclaiming with a beating heart: 'To die will be an awfully big adventure.'

DARK, DOUR AND IMPENETRABLE

Was James Matthew Barrie able to mourn George? Or did death help him to recover in his heart the little boy that he had known in Kensington Gardens?

After the death of the eldest, he clung even more to Michael, 'the dark, dour and impenetrable' as he called him, but Michael changed and escaped from him too, and Barrie dreaded the time when the young man would no longer need him.

The sad child cannot live without his double. Just as he had to renounce having a mother for himself, he always needs a presence to feel that he exists. If the double leaves him, he dies. We can understand why Peter Pan needed the lost boys and why he hated to see them grow up!

After two difficult years at Eton, Michael was hardened, or at least he had composed a nonchalant façade to mask his real feelings, but everyone knew about his depressed state. One of his closest friends, Robert Booth, was convinced of the evil influence that Barrie exerted on the young man:

> Michael took me back to Barrie's flat a number of times, but I always felt uncomfortable there. There was a morbid atmosphere about it. I remember going there one day and it almost overwhelmed me, and I was glad to get away. We were going back to Oxford in Michael's car, and I said, 'It's a relief to get away from that flat', and he said, 'Yes it is.' But the next day he'd be writing to Barrie as usual . . .

The two men established a relationship considered unhealthy by Michael's entourage: not homosexual, but morbid and beyond the limits of ordinary affectivity. When Barrie was in a dark mood, he tended to drag the young man down with him, as Booth related:

> I remember once coming back to the flat with Michael and going into the study, which was empty. We stood around talking for about five minutes, and then I heard someone cough: I turned round and saw Barrie sitting in the inglenook, almost out of sight. He'd been there all the time, just watching us . . . he was an unhealthy little man, Barrie; and when all is said and done, I think Michael and his brothers would have been better off living in poverty than with that odd, morbid little genius.

Did Michael try to escape the claws of his tutor? After Eton, he no longer wanted to continue his studies and dreamed of living as an artist in Paris, like his Du Maurier grandfather. On the contrary, James Barrie wanted Michael to go up to Oxford. It was Michael who finally gave in, to please Barrie, because this was vital for him. As a reward, he was given a car and a little house.

The other Davies children more or less cut themselves off from the writer. At the age of 19, Peter had been sent to the heart of the very worst conflict of the war, the Battle of the Somme. He returned two months later, deeply traumatized, and affected by moral wounds from which he never recovered.

With George dead, and his parents vanished, Peter lived for two years outside of time, filled with fear, obsessed by the memory of mud and mutilated bodies, and he never returned to the Never Land of James Matthew Barrie. He set up house with a woman who was twice his age, and this deeply shocked his tutor, and was opposed by everyone, including Mary Hodgson, who for once agreed with Barrie and shared his disappointment.

Jack also escaped by marrying Geraldine Gibb. Barrie, who maintained a rather bad relationship with the 'intruder', nevertheless used her finally to get rid of Mary Hodgson, the boys' beloved governess. She could not bear the presence of the young wife and never spoke to her directly. Barrie exploited the situation by installing Gerrie as the mistress of the house in Campden Hill Square. He then pretended to ignore the rising tension and wrote to Mary with great tenderness when she offered her resignation. He had won: in the Never Land, one kills or is killed!

HISTORY REPEATS ITSELF

In the summer of 1918, James Barrie had an important new encounter: 'a second chance'? As with Sylvia, it happened during a dinner. The young woman (30 years old, as Sylvia had been at the famous soirée) was Cynthia Asquith. She was married to a solicitor (like Arthur), and was the mother of two boys; Michael, the younger, was the same age as George had been. Cynthia nourished ambitions, especially the desire to make the most of her beauty and her charm. Her husband, who was not very successful professionally, had just abandoned his solicitorship to try his chance in the artistic professions. She needed to earn money. James Barrie offered her a job as a secretary with a high salary and great latitude in her working hours.

Before accepting, she sounded out a number of friends on the writer's personality. She wrote to her friend Sir Walter Raleigh, who answered:

> Why not? But take care you don't kill the golden goose by curbing his sentimentality. Not that it is really sentimentality. It's far more often – for he has a cruel side – satire that doesn't quite come off.

Desmond MacCarthy, another close friend, congratulated her for taking the post:

> It seems to me . . . you like being adored – a Dulcinea is a necessity to Barrie. Sentiment is only irritating to an onlooker, and when it is combined with playfulness and real kindness and springs from a cold detached heart, it is a delicate tactful thing, delightful to receive. Barrie, as I read him, is part mother, part hero-worshipping maiden, part grandfather, and part pixie with no man in him at all. His genius is a coquettish thing, with just a drop of benevolent acid in it sometimes.

The professional relationship between Cynthia and James Barrie was soon transformed into a sincere friendship. But Bob Asquith did not share his wife's admiration for the playwright. He hated his plays and had no sympathy for the man. It is likely that his active resistance (quite different from the resignation of Arthur Davies) and Cynthia's strong personality containing a large dose of egoism prevented history from repeating itself, because James Matthew Barrie never enjoyed over the Asquiths and their children the power that he had over the Davies.

It is true that 'his boys' still occupied a very large place in his life. Michael was pursuing his studies at Oxford, where he had formed a deep friendship with a young man named Rupert Buxton, depressed like himself. Their entourage worried about the influence on Michael of this boy who was exceptionally intelligent, but sombre, saturnine and suicidal.

On Thursday, 19 May 1921, James Barrie was putting on his cloak and hat and was ready to leave the house when he found a reporter from a London daily on his doorstep, requesting an interview on the drowning. The drowning? Two Oxford students, Rupert Buxton and Michael Davies, had just disappeared while swimming in the Thames at Sandford pool. Their bodies had not yet been found, but there had been witnesses. The water was very calm at the time of the accident, and the two boys were in each other's arms. Many people thought it was a double suicide.

The story made the headlines of all the English papers, with eloquent titles and commentaries:

> The tragedy of Peter Pan: Sir JM Barrie's Loss of An Adopted Son: There is something of the wistful pathos of some of his own imaginings in the tragedy which has darkened the home of Sir James Barrie. The young men, Mr Michael Llewelyn Davies and Mr Rupert E V Buxton . . . were drowned near Sandford bathing pool, Oxford, yesterday. The two undergraduates were almost inseparable companions. Mr Davies was only 20 and Mr Buxton 22 . . . The 'original' of Peter Pan was named George, who was killed in action in March 1915 . . . Now both boys who are most closely associated with the fashioning of Peter Pan are dead . . .

After this drama, James Barrie shut himself up and refused to see anyone. Michael was buried in Hampstead cemetery, near the tomb of his parents. A few weeks earlier, Barrie had written in his diary:

> Death: One who died is only a little ahead of procession all moving that way. When we round the corner we'll see him again. We have only lost him for a moment because we fell behind, stopping to tie a shoe-lace.

On 5 April 1960, Peter Llewelyn Davies, publisher, left the Royal Court Hotel, London, crossed Sloane Square, descended the stairs to the underground and threw himself under a train. The tragedy of Peter Pan once again hit the London headlines. James Matthew Barrie's three favourite boys, each in his own way, had lived 'the biggest of all adventures'.

Was it fate? Or did little Jimmy really believe in a 'second chance'? This question always remained at the centre of James Matthew Barrie's thoughts, and it assumed the most varied forms in his plays. In *The Will*, for example:

Purdie: It isn't accident that shapes our lives.
Joanna: No, it's Fate.
Purdie: It's not Fate, Joanna. Fate is something outside us. What really plays the dickens with us is something in ourselves. Something that makes us go on doing the same sort of fool things, however many chances we get . . . Something we are born with . . . Shakespeare knew what he was talking about . . .

> The fault, dear Brutus, is not in our stars,
> But in ourselves, that we are underlings.

7

Folded Wings

One evening when my son was three years old, he said to me, just after the privileged storytime: 'Mummy, I am sad because I know that you and Daddy will die one day. I cannot laugh any more like I used to.' Yet his laughter has never ceased; but at that particular time, something had surely changed for him. And then, some time later, he suddenly exclaimed, with great flippancy: 'Mummy, when you're dead, you'll leave me all your money, won't you?'

It is strange how children can speak so lightly of death. In their games, Wendy and her brothers had no difficulty in imagining that they had encountered their dead father in the forest. Freud finds that only children are capable of speaking of death unrestrainedly and of threatening anyone with death, even those they love. Adults, he says, even if they know that death is the natural culmination of life, sidestep this idea and try to act as if death could be eliminated. Besides, the unconscious is unaware of death; it cannot possibly picture its own end.

We act as though we were immortal, as if nothing could happen. I know today that my father, like many heroes, was convinced of being protected, that the gods were with him. My mother told me about a maxim that always circulated in the family about 'the Kanitz guardian angel'. This may be why our change of name made her so unhappy. The

Kanitz guardian angel was enough for my father; he needed nothing else.

LITTLE CRIMINAL

Where lies the danger? When we think that death is possible? Or, on the contrary, when we find ourselves immortal, among the gods? These feelings perhaps come back to us when we have a real dread of death . . . Is it for fear of wishing to kill a loved one?

A sad child cannot kill like the giant who makes anything he wants disappear, because he has already paid the true price, either having experienced real death, or with the loss of love. For him, losing love is equivalent to losing life; he is faced with the danger of disappearing himself, and he can no longer have the luxury of making others disappear. When he becomes an adult, this child retains deep in himself an inability to love, because he feels guilty of a crime, even if he does not know what it is.

A man came to see me one day. He had recently become a father, but though this made him very happy, he felt an irrepressible need to hurt his baby. This situation made him feel guilty and so desperate that he asked for help, almost threatening me: he was certainly going to end his days in prison. Faced with the urgency of the situation I had to accept, but I also noted my own surprising feelings. I should have retreated before such a contemptible act, and yet I was overcome by a deep sympathy for this man. Besides, I couldn't help seeing the baby in him. . .

He could only feel the surface of his being; in his mind there was the void of his childhood memory. Above all, he hated to be disturbed by noises: horns, fireworks and cars. A violent and unexpected sound could make him lose control, and break out like a madman. His baby's cries also triggered these uncontrollable reactions.

His family had told him that he had had a brother, two years younger, who had died when he himself was four. He had no memory of this, and I had the impression that once again the key lay in forgetting.

The Never Land of this lost child was so far gone that he needed the help of his mother to reach it. It is unusual for mothers to come to me when the lost child is an adult. One day, I received a call from the woman who wanted to tell me something that she had never been able to tell her son and felt that it could help me: 'When the little one died, my husband went mad with grief; he was unrecognizable, he found his older son unbearable, the son he still had, and he said these terrible words: "Why isn't it he who died?" Sometime later, I found my son on a chair, all alone. He was crying and said: "Mummy, will I never see my brother again?" I answered that he must not cry, that his brother was in heaven with the angels and that there were other children in the family, and that we wouldn't talk about it any more.'

I encouraged the old woman to tell the whole story to her son, because he was now an adult, and could therefore bear it. It was mainly to restore something that belonged to him. Alas, the mother was unable to hark back to the years that had elapsed, and she asked me to do it in her place.

When we found ourselves facing the tragic little figure seated alone in his chair, the man burst out sobbing. For the first time, he could weep about his story and he uttered these words: 'My baby! My poor little child, now I understand everything!' The reconstruction of the drama of the child's life had helped this man to experience feelings again. From then on, he managed to overcome the violent urges that assailed him.

TEARS OF ABSENCE

It took years for me to understand that our story had been a tragedy. I was convinced that we had lived through a great adventure, and that my father had died as a hero. My mother, more conservative, said that it was fate. She had her own way of playing with fate; she ceaselessly imagined how things would have transpired 'if only'. If they had left Hungary with my father when she was 20 and he 30 . . . If she had married Zoltan, and not Pista . . . If she had remained in Italy at the age of 19 . . . If she had been born a boy rather than a girl . . . If her mother had let her die . . .

We took long walks on Sundays, during which we spoke of the past and the future. I didn't like the 'ifs'; I found it too sad to have regrets! I preferred 'when': when I grow up . . . when I finish my studies . . . when I have money . . . Then we made plans, I flew off for a thousand adventures and I dragged my mother along with me, where she could find her lost dreams again.

We also cried. At the time, my mother worked hard and she had to leave me alone in the evenings. My brother was often absent. I spent hours in the semi-darkness in the chair where my father used to sit, listening to music. I had a cat who loved Mozart. We consoled each other.

My father died in the spring. It was now winter. It was snowing heavily and my mother had not returned. The hour was late, and I awaited her arrival at the window. The snow covered everything, and a few street lamps cast a bluish light on the immaculate whiteness. Little by little, my tears began to flow, as I gradually became certain that I had also lost my mother. The same tears have returned from time to time in my life, and the feeling of total despair that invaded me then remain, I believe, buried in the depths of the Never Land.

I wept till there were no more tears. Then I distinguished a little black spot, far in the distance, on the snow. It approached rapidly. The little black spot was my mother!

As time passed, we both wept less. Life bore me towards other adventures. My mother henceforth claimed to live only for us. Her life as a woman was finished; she was nothing else but a mother. What did she expect from me? I had taken the place of my father. As he had enjoined me, I took care of her. He had no confidence in my brother.

But how to grow up? How to become a woman? These questions did not concern me; I was too busy finding ways to realize my father's dream: 'Dr Katalin Kanitz'.

Now that he was dead, his dreams about me had become my most cherished possessions. Much later, when I started delving into the Never Land, I found therein the pathetic image of a little girl striking a coffin with all her strength to find what she had lost – my father had taken away with him what I needed to become a woman.

So I took what remained: his dreams, his words, and the memory of his warm hands. My dead father sustained me in my flight towards life. Without knowing it, I drew my strength from the secret contract signed between us. A contract which he could not terminate, because he had become silent and because all the unconscious speech was on my side. I was 'my father's daughter', armed with the desire to conquer the world.

PETER PAN'S BABY TEETH

When a lost child begins to grow up, he is often very responsible, concerned with the well-being of his parents, of his brothers and sisters. You see him at the head of the team, organizing the next game; he picks up the weakest, he has an answer for everything. Above all, if he sees someone despondent, depressed, resourceless, the lost child runs to help him, to try to cheer him up. The lost child becomes a social worker, the lost child becomes a doctor, the lost child becomes a psychoanalyst.

Who can say that the lost child has not grown up? He is independent, he is full of energy, he is the parent of his parents . . . Yet if a smile is closely scrutinized, one finds that he still has his baby teeth!

When I was 16, I was earning a living and saving for my university studies. I did theatre, I had many friends, and I was happy to be alive. I had romantic affairs, enough for my taste and to nourish my mother with my reports. I told her everything; she participated fully in my life. The only dark spot in my existence was our relationship with my brother and his wife.

After my father died, my mother, not having enough courage to start a life alone with me, had agreed to share my brother's house. Little by little, the situation became untenable and yet it lasted. My brother was very violent at times, and I learned to fear and hate him.

Did he feel that he had to replace my father? I had two men in my life: a dead hero, enclosed in my heart, and a living devil in real life. This dual situation surely sustained the Never Land deep within me, and did not facilitate my capacity to grow up.

Freud has shown that the little girl, in love with her father, expects him to give her a child; but she finally realizes that this is an impossible dream and that she has to give up this hope and find another man, who will love her and whose child she will bear. This is essential for the little girl to become a woman.

But when a father dies before his little girl can let go of this hope, she may be so violently disappointed that she has no alternative but to lock this dream for ever in the Never Land, in order that the violent feelings will not destroy everything, including herself. I reserved my anger and hatred for my brother, because he had such talent to attract them; thus I could dream of a hero that I would meet one day somewhere else, I knew not where . . .

I think that I have always known that I would leave Canada one day and return to Europe, even if a return to Hungary was impossible. Hungary was the place of the Never Land, which I filled with all my childhood dreams and which I nourished with my mother's stories. It was a

distant country, far beyond China, beyond the planet Mars .
. . I knew that I had to return to the east, to recross the Atlantic,
discover France . . . I did not yet know that once again I was
turning to the past to find what I had lost . . .

The beginning of my stay in Paris was extremely pleasant:
everything attracted me – the smells, the colours, the people,
the street corners, the words. I had come over to learn French,
and the language would finally unite two separate parts in
me, the English head and the Hungarian heart, thanks to
which I started to talk about myself, to think and to feel at
the same time.

I found the members of my father's family. I felt that I was
visiting a part of the Never Land; at the time, it was filled
with the most varied things, good and bad – I had not put
anything in order! So when something was good, everything
was good. In France, everything was good.

The fact that I had changed countries and had placed an
ocean between my mother and myself certainly gave me the
impression of growing up. This is often the strategy of the sad
child: to leave home and venture far away and to return
transformed, adult, without having been forced to experience the painful separation every day. Flying off in this way
unwittingly enabled me to retain deep nostalgia for my
mother and to continue on the road that my father had made
us take: the road to the Never Land.

Toronto . . . Paris . . . Geneva . . . All exiles some day land
in Geneva. Switzerland: clean and organized, strange and
mysterious, unbearable . . . I knew no one in Geneva, I lived
alone and it was up to me to build my life. Did I have to go
that far to escape from parental desire and find myself?

I could still flee. But something prevented me from letting
go. And what 'if the difficulty of living were the biggest
adventure of all'? I was obstinate, I would not give up. But
in Switzerland I lived through moments of solitude, of
despair, spasms of tears, as before . . .

THE ISLE OF ORIGINS

I do not know how the idea of going to see a 'passer' came to me. For the first time, I realized that I was sad and that something weighed on my story; adventures were not enough, I wanted the truth, my truth. Only I needed to speak in my mother tongue, because the key to the Never Land lies in the hollow of the earliest words.

'What can I do for you?' he asked me. He looked and sounded like someone I had known a long time ago. He was bald, like my father, and he rolled his 'rs' . . . that was good.

But I was scared, I did not want to do an 'analysis' as they say, nor anything very long, or very expensive . . . just enough to . . . Strange, this man behind me who said nothing. He does it on purpose. I cannot cross the border of intimacy, I am unable to speak to him in Hungarian. Yet one day, without any apparent reason, and without even realizing it, I used my ancestral language. The dreams start flowing as from a secret spring unknown to me. Dreams of a large and dark apartment where I see two birds painted on the ceiling, signs of fate, a house cut in two, the revolution, a bomb, I bleed, my mother runs to help me . . .

What do I expect from the 'passer'? His silences let me progress at my own pace. But he is not always silent. He tries to point out the road, he offers me some keys. Can I understand the enigma of my story? The Never Land opens before me, especially at night. I am at the Hungarian border. No one knows it yet, but there is a war on between the French and the Americans. There are a great number of tents and I am in the middle. The soldiers are killing each other, but I succeed in escaping, thanks to a bomb which I clasp in my hand! I hide behind a tent. I am in a forest and I meet my father. He had left long before and, this time, it's true, it's not a dream, but he is ill, he has to be careful because he will probably die; we have very little time to spend together and we have things of the greatest importance to tell each other.

But what were we speaking of? I don't know . . . I wake with the feeling of his presence strongly embedded in me. And then comes the tiredness, the greyness, the nostalgia for the absolute . . .

The old notebooks of the Swiss period contain notes written at very different times; dreams, thoughts, cries of solitude. And then two curious pages which I cannot remember having written:

> She tried, but the words would not come, could not come. He loved her, he had said it, he had written it: 'Please, only a few lines, if you knew how your silence hurts me.' As a child, as she had often asked herself whether one could simply jump out of one's skin, leave everything and start over. 'If I were not I . . . ?' No one could answer her.
>
> One day it happened. It frightened her at first, but, little by little, the feeling became pleasant, a powerful feeling of freedom. She had succeeded in leaving her body.
>
> Subsequently, she often succeeded in provoking this feeling of absence/presence, even when she was in the company of others. It was as if she saw everything from very far, the bodies, words and gestures lost their meaning. Nothing had any meaning and she seemed to float in a very pleasant vacuum.
>
> But, at about the age of sixteen, she lost this gift. At present, it was no more than a memory.

It is strange that this text should fall into my hands, as I now write . . . That I finally agree to fold my wings to examine the Never Land of my story. To fix words, to take images designed to persist, is a way to kill . . . to accept that the Never Land will emerge from the shadows, that the past is past and that what is lost is lost for ever . . .

I understand today that this text, written 20 years ago, was already addressed to my father. The word impossible to say was the word 'Farewell', farewell to my father.

I now write it on these pages, and I no longer tear them up, but I offer them to the memory of a lost childhood . . .